SURPRISE,
I AM STILL HERE,
TO TELL MY STORY,
AFTER MANY YEARS

ROBERT RAY SWAN

ISBN 978-1-0980-8840-8 (paperback)
ISBN 978-1-0980-8924-5 (digital)

Christian Faith Publishing, Inc.
832 Park Avenue
Meadville, PA 16335
www.christianfaithpublishing.com

Printed in the United States of America

CONTENTS

SURPRISE, I AM STILL HERE,
TO TELL MY STORY, AFTER MANY YEARS

My book is called *SURPRISE, I AM STILL HERE, TO TELL MY STORY, AFTER SO MANY YEARS*. It is about a soldier that was from a small farming community of Iowa. I was born in the late forties and had some serious issues as a young child. I got into trouble at school several times as a child but turned out to be a pretty bright kid.

As I was about to go off to college, the draft chose me first. I was number one on the draft in my hometown of Albia, Iowa, in 1967. I was given the chance to enlist into the military of my choice or be drafted within the week. I decided to enlist into the medical field of the US Army after taking some qualifying tests and getting above a 120 score. I scored 149. I was told I would be going to Fort Polk in Louisiana, Texas for basic training and then to Fort Sam Houston in San Antonio, Texas for med school 91B. Then I would be transferred to Travis Air Force Base then off to Vietnam for one years. Read and enjoy.

My name is Robert Ray Swan. I am seventy-one years old and am just now telling the story of my life and adventure into the great war of all wars, in my opinion. I am writing this book after many hours of therapy that the VA Health Care has given to me by the Veteran Administration Hospitals in several locations in the United States. If it were not for the VA and all those who helped get to this point in my life, I would not be here today doing this, so I thank them very much. I also thank all those who supported me and encouraged me to write this book. I am not the same person I was in 1967–1968 when I graduated from Albia Community High School in Albia, Iowa. I just attended my fiftieth class reunion, and they were all in support of me going on with my book. They had all been notified that I had been killed in action in 1969. Indeed, they were all shocked to see me when I showed up at the reunion still alive and attending the reunion.

When I showed up at the reunion, several of the closer students I hung around with, well the students I knew, were so shocked that they cried and almost fainted with so much emotional shock. They said to write the book so they could get a copy. So here is the book and what the title tells about is that it is a surprise that I made it home to be able to tell my story to the world. I hope you enjoy it as much as I enjoyed writing it.

It brought back a lot of memories I have been trying to forget for a long time. It has been a long time since I have been there. I will explain as much as I can. If I seem confused or disoriented, it may be. Some of the things I say may sound strange or gross, but it is true. It is not easy to talk about how you handle yourself under hostile combat and bloody emotional conditions. The situations you get into is quite awful at times. I will go into it more in detail as the book goes on.

I do thank all my family also who also helped me try and stay focused so I could think of what to write. They also reminded me of who I was and what I had achieved in my lifetime. My success as a person as well as a soldier shows greatly by all the ribbons and stripes I earned. I will begin my book by starting at the beginning of my life because it was not the greatest. It was quite unusual for a person such as me. I will do my best to explain what I mean as you will see in the beginning chapters of the book.

I was an unusual child and was treated rather differently from other little boys of my gender at that time and age group as you will read about. Do not let this hinder you from following through with the book for it gets much better as it goes along for me as I grew up and become who I was destined to be. Please read the book and you will see how I do develop into quite a success or failure in life. Decide for yourself whether my life became, in your opinion, what it should or should not have been.

CHAPTER 1

The Beginning

It was an early June summer morning. There was a warm, moist breeze in the air coming off the Mississippi River over the city of Oskaloosa, Mahaska County, Iowa. The blossoms were blowing around like little tornados in the breeze. It was June 27, 1949, and the time was about 4:34 a.m. Everyone was in bed asleep after a restless evening the night before. Mom was having labor pains and could not get any sleep. She finally went to sleep at midnight according to Carol, the oldest daughter in the house. At 4:30 a.m., my mother, Naomi Jenny (Kirby) Swan, woke up with a sharp pain again in her lower abdominal areas.

My dad, Oscar Orville Swan, jumped into action this time. He was well-aware of what was going on. He hurriedly dressed and got my mother ready to go to the hospital. He woke the rest of the children up and told them that their mother was in labor for sure this time and he was taking her to the hospital. He told the other children they were to stay there and wait for his call. At the time, Carol and David were there at home. He called the neighbors to come and keep an eye out for the two children at home, which they said they gladly would do and came right over.

On the way to the hospital, Mother was placed in the back seat of Dad's beat up four-door pick-up truck lying down. She was having contractions and some pain. It took about fifteen to twenty minutes to get to the hospital. Dad was worried that something might be wrong with his wife, so he said a little prayer on the way to the hospital. It seemed to calm Mother down. When they arrived at the hospital, the medical staff was waiting for her. They rushed Mrs. Swan into one of the labor and delivery rooms and started their initial preparations for childbirth. It was about 5:00 a.m., and the doctor had just arrived at the hospital.

With his initial look at Mrs. Naomi (Kirby) Swan, the doctor could tell it would not be long before the baby would arrive. Oscar was able to go into the room where Mrs. Swan was so he could observe the birth, but he wanted no part in that and was soon escorted to the waiting room because he said he would get sick at the sight of birth. So he was hesitant of seeing the birth of his baby. It was at 6:45 a.m. when the baby arrived.

Mrs. Naomi Jenny (Kirby) Swan had a baby boy. She called him Robert Ray Swan. She was disappointed somewhat because she thought she was going to have a girl. She was glad that I, the baby, was healthy and had lots of hair. The nurse took me, the baby, immediately away to clean me up and check me out while the doctor finished cleaning Mrs. Swan up and getting her ready to receive her baby. She was quite sore and had to have some stitches put in place to stop some bleeding that was going on. They said this was normal. I, the baby, was brought back to my mother's waiting arms, and I was reported as doing great. Mother and I were released from hospital after three days, which was normal back in the forties. She left the hospital in a wheelchair because of hospital regulations.

I was told I grew up with having a lot of crying spells, and Dad got angry that he was being kept up at night and he had to get up early to go to work in the mornings. One time he got so angry that he tried throwing me out the window. If Mom had not been there and grabbed my legs, I, Robert, would have been out the window.

Mom pampered me so much and called me her little angel. See, Mom wanted a girl. She treated me like as if I, Robert, were a girl quite a bit of the time as I grew up as a little child. She dressed me most of the time up in little girl's clothes and called me always her pretty little girl. My mother would put bows in the hair and the whole ball of wax a few times just because I did have a lot of long hair. All the neighbors thought that I really was a little girl. She started calling me Roberta at times.

I was told I was a very active child but had a bad habit of being scared all the time. I was told that I would start crying over a lot of things around me. I was even afraid of the dogs and cats that were around me. I was even afraid of my brother and sister most of the times. I did like to go on car and truck rides. That would settle me down quite a lot. I also even liked it when someone would comb my long blondish brown hair.

To a lot of people, they thought that I was growing up too fast. The first five years went by really fast. Mom was still trying to dress me in girl's clothes till one day, Dad put his foot down and told mom she had a boy, not a girl. Mom got some hand me down clothes of my brother and started dressing me or teaching me to dress as a boy. I seemed to start warring baggy overhauls with a t-shirt of sort till I started school.

I, Robert, had several brothers and sisters as I was growing up in my life. The family got to be a pretty big size with a total of eleven children plus two parents. The oldest child was a half-brother named Jackson Junior Swan born in 1933. The second was a half-brother named Kenneth Emanuel Swan born in 1935. Then there was an older sister named Carol Ellen Swan born in 1945. Then came David Dewayne Swan born in 1947. Then came me, Robert Ray Swan, born in 1949. Some people say 1948, but my birth certificate says 1949. It's smudged and hard to read. I really do not know for sure about the real year.

I will also at this time name the other brother and sisters of the Swan family. The next in line was a girl named Constance (Connie) Sue Swan born in 1951. Then came Stephen Sydney Swan born in 1953. Then there was Geoffrey Guy Swan. He was next, born in 1955. Then came Treasa Annetta Swan, another sister, born in 1957. Thomas Terrance Swan came next and was born in 1959. He was followed by Bradley Brian Swan born in 1961. Then there was another who was another stepbrother born in 1969, William Wayne Bristol (Billy).

The family lived in several places before I was born, and I can't remember them all, so I will start at when I, Robert, was a child. As I said before, I was born in Oskaloosa, Mahaska, Iowa on June 27, 1949 at the Oskaloosa Hospital at 6:15 a.m. by Dr. Robert Collison, MD. I was told I was eight pounds six ounces and twenty-one inches long at birth. I was a normal size baby as a baby goes. I was told I had somewhat jaundice at birth but cleared up in just a day or two with treatment. I also had some trouble gaining weight as an infant. I, as a baby, was put on formula as well as breast milk so I hopefully would gain weight. It was slow going for a while, but I did start gaining weight like I should.

As was said before, mom treated me most of the time like a little girl and cuddled me a lot up close to her and put little dresses on me quite often. One day, I, out of nowhere, broke out in a rash that looked pretty bad. It looked like there were three different kinds of rings all over his body. She took me, her angel, to the doctor, and they put me immediately into an isolation room. The doctor decided to keep me in the hospital for a week to run tests to see what was wrong with me. When Mom and I got to come home, Mom said that I seem to have had a skin dermatitis of multiple kinds, which was caused by an infection in the blood. I, then, was given medicine, and they said I most likely would clear up in about two to three weeks. If not, I might or would have to have a blood transfusion. I did end up having the blood transfusions before I cleared up. I, then, was put back in the hospital for another week for observation to make sure I would clear up from the infection in my blood.

With the problems I seem to have had as a small child, it somehow affected me somewhat as I was getting bigger. I just was not as big as the other kids my own age. I just was not as strong as the other kids. I just could not play outside games as well as the other kids my own age. It seemed that I even had a hard time playing with my own brothers and sisters. I was told I acted more like a sissy than a rough boy. I seemed and appeared immature for my own age, and it really seemed like that the girlish characteristics had entered me more that my mom started when I was just a little kid.

I was growing up and about ready to start kindergarten, and I appeared like I still wanted to put on dresses and I even, half the time, still wanted to play with dolls. What would the school think of the situation I had got myself in? It was going to take some work to get me somewhat ready to go to school for I had not been away from Mom or the family at all. I even was still a bed wetter and had a hard time controlling my wetting myself many a times during the day. Several people had to remind me all the time to go to the bathroom. I just would go to the bathroom because they told me to go, and sure enough, I would have to go.

I did finally start going on my own, and my family and friends gave me a lot of prayers for it. I did not have to wear dippers any longer, and that made me really feel like I really was growing up. I did start wearing boys' clothing and hand-me-downs, but I seem to start looking like a handsome boy finally. Mom did not like it but knew that she had to let me really be who I was destined to be, and that was a growing boy. So from that point on after, Dad got on Mom's case so she let me grow to be who I really was supposed to be.

This process took about five years to settle, but it was finally over, and my parents thought I appeared like I was finally ready for kindergarten school. They finally registered me in Lincoln Elementary School. It was a half-day kindergarten program. They thought it would be a good program to get me prepared and ready for the first grade. Were they ever wrong!

It seemed I did not do very well in the kindergarten program. They said I appeared that I was slow and immature for my own age group. You might say I did not or look ready to move into the first grade, so they failed me in the kindergarten program, and they told me I would have to retake it again the next year. The next year I did pass in great shape. I appeared I was much more mature and was able to handle the material as it was put before me of anything they offered in that age category. What is so funny is that was the only grade out of all the schooling I had ever took that I really failed in my entire life, and that is including college classes.

From first grade on, I was improving, and I started getting above average grades from then on.

Now that I appeared that I was a little more grown up, that did not mean my behavior had improved. I found myself doing bad things and was still getting into trouble with the other kids in several of my classes. The trouble I got in was sometimes caused by me, and some of it was by caused by the fault of someone else. It was not always started by me. I got in trouble anyway. I seem to have spent a lot of time sitting in the corner. I did have a habit of wanting to sit on the back of my chair with my feet in the chair. I often would tip the chair over several times a day. I was real lucky I did not seriously hurt myself. I sometimes did it to just disturb the class. The teacher would write notes home all the time about my disruptive actions even while I was attending kindergarten. That is one reason why she said I appeared like I was just too immature to start school.

The summer after I failed kindergarten, I was very upset because all my close friends at school had passed except for me. They teased me all the time and said I seemed that I was a sissy and could not do anything right and if I really was going to pass the next year, I needed to learn how I was going to act and know I have to grow up and behave like I really should. A little girl told me in secret that she liked me some but I really needed to be a better person so the other would like me some too. I let her know and told her class that I promise I would be the best in the class next year and surprise everyone, and that is just what I really tried to do.

I put all my effort into getting the highest marks than anyone in the class. It really did help because I passed in flying colors. I tried to do my best so I could keep my promise to the class I was with before, and I did so good the second time around in kindergarten that they advanced me, yes, up to the second grade with my own age group for the next year. So I got to skip the first year of school. I cried because I was so elated and happy that I made it back with my own class and friends and that I had proven to them I really was not a dummy and was as smart as any of them if I put forth the effort and applied myself and did my work like I knew I could just like the other kid in my class. My original class was excited for me, and my little girl friend said, "I knew you could do it, and we can help each other now."

One day, our class were all out playing ball, and I guess I was not paying attention because I was running after a fast ball trying to catch it, and I accidently ran dead into a pole that was sticking out of the ground about four to five feet in the air. It knocked me totally out for a few minutes and put a pretty good size goose egg on my big fat forehead. When I woke, I was dizzy as I could be. Kids came running to help me and managed to struggle to get me up. I then was taken to the nurse by some of the other kids who saw me and held me get to the nurses office, who in turn, called one of my parents to come and get me and to take me to the doctor, which they did.

I appeared to have or had a concussion from the hit on the pole. The school was told that I had a concussion and I was to stay home from school for a week. When I was over with the week at home, I returned to school. They watched over me just for a while longer to make sure I really would be alright. I looked to them and appeared to be a tough kid now. I still was getting into all kinds of scrapes and bruises from somewhere while I was in school. I would think that by guessing, it was just part of my nature of having some kind of scrape or bruise on me.

In 1956, my mother and older sister, Carol, and my older brother, David, got interested in the Church of Jesus

Christ of Latter Day Saints. We had two missionaries, Elder Farms Worth and Elder Williams. I believe that was their names. They were needing a place to live for a while while they were on their missions. My dad was not a religious man, but he saw something in those two young men that others could or would not have seen: honesty and spirituality.

He took to them with a love just like they were his own children. I know Dad was touched by the spirit each time they talked to him about the Gospel and the church. He let them move into our attic apartment rent-free for two years. My dad was not baptized at that time, but he did believe the words they preached. My mother and older sister, Carol, and David were baptized, I believe, early June of 1956. I also joined the church and was baptized on August 3, 1957. You had to be at least eight years old to get baptized. We all got baptized in the Des Moines, Iowa District, but in Ames, Iowa. Ames is a stake to itself now.

We did not have a baptismal font in the Oskaloosa branch at the time. So we went to Ames to get baptized. We had a situation while the missionaries were staying in the attic apartment. One day, we had a hailstorm come into Oskaloosa, Iowa. It was the biggest I had ever seen. We had hail stones the size of soft balls hit the next-door neighbors' roof and were bouncing off and coming through our upstairs window. My brother David, and I, Robert, went upstairs with ball bats and was trying to hit the balls of ice back out the window and really broke more of the windows while doing so than what was done by the ball of ice to start. Did we ever get into trouble when Mom and Dad found out what we had been doing? The missionaries just seem to take it in stride and help fix the windows that were broken. They did a pretty good job too. Dad did not even ask them to do it. He thanked them for their work and took them out to dinner but left David and me home since it was our fault in the first place.

While I was a student at Lincoln School, I still was in a lot of little fights but nothing bad. I do remember my mother putting me in Cub Scouts in a troop from our church. It was quite interesting, and we did learn all sorts of new things. We even got to go out on a father-and-son overnight camp out in Cub Scouts once I remember. I was a Webelos Scout at the time. My dad could not go because he was in a wheelchair, so I had a substitute dad for that night. I was okay with it, and my real dad was okay with it too. He would have went if he could. I understood his disability. He did help me in my scouting activities when he was able to do so. I did get several badges while in Cub Scouts and Webelos Scout and Boy Scouts. One thing I learned how to do but to this day that I am still hesitant in doing is swimming. More so now that the years have gone by and I have got several medical conditions that would really hinder my swimming ability. I get scared to get in water over my head. More about that later when I reveal another situation that water over my head scared me deeply.

I did get my swimming merit badge when our Cub Pack went to a lake for summer camp. We had to swim out to a pier about three hundred feet away, climb up on top of it, jump off, and swim back to shore. I was quite scared, but I knelt down on my knees in front of everyone and said a prayer to the Lord that he would help me so someday I might be able to help some-one else out of trouble swimming. I asked him to help me pass the test so I could help others that feared the water like me. I did pass the test and was able to show all the other cubs that all you really need is faith in the Lord and yourself, and you can do a lot of things.

SURPRISE, I AM STILL HERE,
TO TELL MY STORY, AFTER MANY YEARS

There was a time that I, Robert, had my very wits almost knocked out of my internal soul, and I, Robert, was not very old at the time. I should not have, but I had been playing around the backyard with my bigger brother, David, and we had or were trying to get in the old garage out by the alley about 250 or so yards from the house. The garage was locked, so we were going to see if any of the windows were unlocked. The windows were locked too. I, Robert, had this dumb idea that we together might get a rope or strong string and from the roof, we together might be able to let it down with a loop on the end of it and let it slide through the crack at the top of the garage door. Then I thought we might hock the door latch and pull up on it and unlock the door.

We got everything ready, and I, Robert, started climbing because David was too chicken to do so onto the roof of the garage. Oh, I forgot to say the garage was about a hundred years old. When I managed to get myself up and I got on top of the roof, I crawled on my hands and knees and got to the center or close to the center where I then thought I really might lay down to drop the rope or string. I heard a loud cracking sound coming from the roof, and the next thing that happened was I apparently had went through the roof and was hanging with my arms outside the roof and was suspended in mid-air inside the garage.

David was laughing so hard. It was so funny to him. David went running to the house to get Carol and Dad so they could help get me out of this situation. When Carol and Dad showed up, they were not in a good mood. They saw me dangling from the roof, so Carol then unlocked the garage as fast as she could, and they all went in. There were car parts scattered all over the floor where Dad had been working on putting a car back together. If I had fallen all the way through, I really could have landed right in the center of car parts or in the engine compartment of the car itself. I was told that I could have been real seriously injured.

My Dad was really upset at me for doing what I did, and that was that. I tried getting on the roof at all as young as I was. It was a struggle to get me down without getting me injured further than I was already. My arms were bleeding. I learned a very good lesson from that foolish episode that day. The good Lord was with me and my misbehavior that day. Thank God for it could have been a whole lot worse. Dad had to have the roof fixed, and it cost him better than eight hundred dollars and had to pay a repair man to come out to do the job. So it was better than a thousand dollars total to fix the roof, and I knew I would have to do work and do chores to pay Dad back the money to fix and repair the roof.

It was only fair since I was the main cause the damage. I worked and did chores around the house for several months as well as help cut grass with my bigger brother, David, and pick up leaves and trash around the neighborhood for people to earn extra money to pay my roof debt off. I earned money, paid it toward my debt, and got it paid off in about six months when Dad said I showed I had proven that I really had done enough to show I stepped forward and had really tried to do my true honest part. So Dad said my roof debt was paid in full.

I began started liking school and getting higher grades. I had a favorite teacher. I believe it was in the fourth grade. His name was Mr. Wilson, and he was my history teacher. He was fair but honest with all his students. He did not take any bull from anyone. I think he was the best teacher I, in my opinion, ever had and respected, and I really worked hard for. He also substituted in science, which I really liked a lot also. With Mr. Wilson's encouragement and making sure, I did things by the books.

I managed to build one of the best replicas of the solar system the school had ever seen. I worked hard on it. Mr. Wilson encouraged me to take it to the state science fair. I did, and I got a Superior Outstanding First Place Ribbon for Over All Excellence. They even kept it to store for future shows. I was involved in another project also with Mr. Wilson's guidance, not doing the work but making sure it was done correctly. I managed to build a scale model three feet by three feet of an atomic pile reactor. I fixed it up or had it ridged up, so it worked but with minimal current so it would not cause a fire or explosion. It had just enough current to light up some small Christmas tree-type lights inside, which were attached to my own atom rods I had inside the reactor. The light would flash on and off as the current was going through the rods. This showed that energy was being produced. I received also a superior Outstanding Over All Excellence ribbon at the state science fair. Mr. Wilson told me I had a good head on my shoulders and was one of his best students he had ever had. It made me feel very proud to have known such a person. He will always be remembered. I would have to say that Mr. Wilson would have to be my inspiration or person who I would most likely pattern my life after.

Section 2: Grade School and Move to Montana and Back to Eddyville, Iowa

This first part of my book may not seem like that it is drawing me into being a soldier, but everything I apparently would learn and grow to achieve would help me really become the soldier I would become and want to be.

When I got to Helena, Montana, I found out I had an uncle and an aunt and four cousins. Gowan Guy Kirby was my uncle's name, and Fran was my aunt's name. They had two daughters, Gwen and Mona Kirby. They also had two sons named Bill and Bob Kokoruda according to their birth records. Their last names were change to Kirby when my uncle, Gowan Kirby, adopted them when they came to live with them. The boys then became related to Gowan and his family and to my mother. Gowan and Naomi Jenny Kirby (Swan), my mother, were brother and sister.

Our family moved out of town about twelve miles from Helena, Montana, and up on a mountain two miles up to a pretty quaint but far out four-bedroom house. It did not have running water. We had to haul water from a well over a half mile up the mountain side and back and down to the house. It had a wood burning pot belly stove for heat in the living room and a gas stove in the kitchen to cook on. We had to use an outside toilet, and we were not used to it.

The mine that Dad bought was about one and three fourths of a mile further up the mountain following the winding road. The mine was about two to three miles long and had seats and lights scattered along the inside so you could sit and look at the site of the inside of the mine. There were restrooms and drinking fountains in several locations. There were also some soda machines located throughout the mine for those who wanted one. There was reading material on several different illnesses that uranium was good in the treatment for. So the uranium was supposed to be good for your health. This brought in a lot of people into the mine daily.

Dad bought the mine because he thought he could cure himself of MS and be able to walk better with the treatment at the mine. It did help some while he was there, but it did not seem to have any lasting effect on him. Others said it did wonders on them. I believe that Dad was in the last stage of his MS disease. It did help him for the four years we were there. I know I walked through the mine every day for four years and stayed for two hours each day, and I think I was able to build a resistance to some diseases that I could have gotten that would have made matters worse.

We had to go to Helena to go to school. I attended C R Anderson Elementary and Middle School. I did not care for the school or the classmates to start with. I had trouble from the start. I found myself sitting out in the hall on many occasions. I even threw a rubber boot at the teacher because she asked me of all people not to wear them in the classroom. I told her I was not take them off, did not want anyone to steal them, so I was going to wear them. She sent me out, so I got mad and took my boots off and threw them at her. I made a mistake and did not get them back the rest of the year.

I did begin and finally settled down and started adjusting well to the western way of doing things. I became a quite honest and polite young man. I even started singing in the choir and doing a pretty good job. They let me sing a solo at a state music contest. I shocked everyone and got an outstanding superior rating. My song was a religious song called "I Believe." I had bad experience in that I was in music class in 1963 when an announcement came over the loud speaker that President John F. Kennedy had been assassinated in Dallas, Texas. The whole class was in shock and could not function anymore that day. School was dismissed, and parents were called to come and pick up their children. This was also about the same time my parents split up, and my mother and all the children moved to town. We moved into a smaller house in town, but it had indoor plumbing. My dad moved back to Newton, Iowa, and my oldest brother helped him purchase a school bus and convert it into a livable trailer dwelling. He then moved him into a house about two years later.

Back in Helena, where we moved to, for some reason, our cousins did not live too far away because we were able to play and talk every day with them. We still went to the same school. There were a lot of kids driving cars in the area where we lived. They would drive fast and at times try and scare the kids that were walking on the edge of the road. My brother and I, Robert, and some of the neighbor boys got together one night. We devised a plan and that we would get some rocks and hide out up and down the long stretch of road waiting for those speeders to come by and when they did, we were going to throw rocks at their cars and take off to teach them to slow down. Those speeders just jumped out of their cars and tried to catch us, but luckily, they did not catch anyone. They did slow down coming through the area from then on.

Since I did not know the area very well, I went looking around all the time. I noticed an alley running along the side of our property, and I would walk down it to see what was down it. There were several buildings. They must have been apartments. Further down, there was another cross street. There were all kinds of stores. One day as I was venturing out, I saw what I thought was a gas truck parked in the alley. I was about to find out when I saw a boy start climbing up onto the gas truck. I yelled out, "What are you doing?"

As the boy got to the top, he looked at me and said he was going to see if there was gas in the truck. I told him, "Do not check because something could go wrong!" The next thing I knew was that the kid opened a hatch door and lit a match to look in. The truck exploded, and the kid was thrown a good a hundred feet toward me. I took my shirt off and tried to put out the flames on his body and tried to give him mouth-to-mouth. People came running to help. Someone called 911.

In just a short time, there was an ambulance and police and fire trucks there to take over. I had continued to give mouth-to-mouth till the paramedics got there. When they saw me, they were so astonished that I, so young, would know how to give mouth-to-mouth. The boy lived but had 75 percent burns all over his body. They said if it were not for me being there when I was, he would have died. He was in the hospital for a couple of years having skin grafts done. To this day, I always think it could have been me if I would have had not of seen him climbing on that gas truck. Another one of God's miracles we do not think about that happen in our lives. Thank goodness for the little bit of training I had in scouts they gave us. It helped me to help someone else live longer after a serious accident. It was also God's will that he would live and that I just was there to help in some little way and all the others who came to the rescue.

I remember one time I was bad and played a mean trick on a couple of teenagers living in the area. We had a tree outside our yard and down the alley just a little way. One day I remember that I decided to climb the tree because I was mad at my brother and sister. You might say I was hiding from them. I remember I got some food from the house and a blanket because I really thought I was going to be up the tree for a little while. Oh yes, I did also take a pack of Dad's cigarettes and matches with me. I know I had never had a cigarette or smoked one, but Mom had some of them lying on the mantle. I guess I figured Carol or David would get the blame for taking them.

I managed to climb the tree, which was about twenty feet high. I thought I was pretty well hidden from all the leaves and branches from the tree. It was about supper time because I, from a distance, heard someone calling me for supper. I kept quiet and did not make a sound, and finally, they went back in the house. While I was eating some food, I saw or noticed a teenage couple walking toward the tree. I tried to stay real still. I started to watch them sit down under the tree in the fuzzy warm grass blowing ever so slowly in the breeze, like a bed under the tree limbs on the ground.

They sat there talking for a while about school and other things that did not interest me at all. I just could tell they were up to something. They started smoking cigarettes, and the aroma lingered gently upward toward me, filling the air through the leaves of the tree causing the air to stink, and it was making me sick to my stomach. I was really wanted to throw up, but they were under the tree. They laid down, and it was starting to get dark out now, so it was getting harder to see. But there was one streetlight about ten to fifteen feet away from where we were at. They took their clothes off and was going to get it on, but I decided it was not going to happen. I began to light a cigarette and almost choked but was able to clear my throat okay, so I did get in a position where I thought I could drop the cigarette down between the legs of the guy.

I apparently missed and put it between the girl legs. She let out a scream, and the guy could not figure what was wrong. She told him she was burned by a cigarette between her legs. They looked up in the tree and saw me, and I really was so scared I scrambled and got out of the tree so fast and got over our fence in our yard. The guy and girl, well, they did not even get fully dressed. I hurried and went through the back door before they got to the house.

When they knocked on the door and my mother answered it, I really thought I would be punished big time. My mother asked the girl how on earth she was burnt by a cigarette between her legs and what she was doing to have that done to her. My mother started laughing and told her she should keep her clothes on and not be lying under trees because you never know what might be in them. Mom smiled at me and only said stay out of the trees.

There was one other incident that happened that was worth mentioning. I told you I said I did not know the area too well where we lived. The longer we lived there, and I began to search the area out. I was amazed that I found out that we did not live to far from our cousins, Gwen and Mona Kirby. Mona was about my age and at the time appeared to be a cute girl. She became a very close friend to me. We hung out all the time. People thought we were a couple, and we just laughed it off. But one day, we were caught sitting under the front end of a trailer truck kissing.

That was the first girl I really had ever kissed, and I was scared she was going to hit me. But she did not. She wanted me to, she said. We were called later the kissing cousins. She died a couple of months ago, and it felt like a part of me died with her. She will be sorely missed. She will always be a dear friend to me always and that I will cherish and shall remember forever.

She kept me out of a lot of fights at school and helped me to grow up and be a more responsible person and a much better student academically. She helped me so I was able and could achieve my first A on a test in middle school by studying extra hard and applying myself properly and not acting stupid like I seem to have been doing. It paid off, and I did start getting more As and a big smile from Mona who said, "I told you could do it if you tried."

Section 3: Teenage Years and High School

We moved back to Eddyville, Iowa, in 1964 to a house out in the country about five to ten miles out of town. We had only one neighbor, Mr. Johnson (name changed to protect his privacy). He was an old Irish man, and he lived with his son, Troy. They were trying to work a small farm and doing what I assumed or thought was a good job. Their place was clean and mowed and looked in great shape. They had a few sheep grazing on about a hundred acres of prime land. They did a lot of hard work to keep it looking that way.

Our place was an older two-story home on three to five acres of land. We had a pot belly stove in the living room for heat and a wood burning stove in the kitchen for cooking. We had to go outside to an outhouse to go to the bathroom again. It was about a mile walk to one of our uncles, Norval's Kirby, another one of my mother's brother's fields where he planted corn.

I remember one day my brother and sister and I decided to take a walk, and we went to see Uncle Norval at work. He was in his field with some strange tanks putting spray on the ground. I did not know the situation of the type of farming he was doing. I ran up toward him, and he did not see me coming at first. As I began to approach or got closer to him, I immediately started gasping for air and hit the ground like I was rotting the soil like an animal. When my Uncle Norval saw me, he immediately shut his tanks off and came running to me to help me start breath again. He gave me a lesson on ammonium nitrate oxide and what it can do to a person who breaths too much of it in at once. He had a mask on when he was spraying. It took about ten minutes to get my normal breathing back. He put a mask on me and ran some oxygen through it so I could start breathing once again on my own.

That was the last time I ever went to his fields when he had the tanks out.

We attended school at Eddyville for about six to seven months before we decided to move to Albia, Iowa. We got a house one block from the high school. It was located at 523 B Ave E. It did not take long to make friends or to find out who the rich kids or most popular kids were—the ones who got everything first and who got what was left, if you were lucky enough to get it. That was my feeling toward the school. Else why would you choose a freshman and put him on the varsity football team when you have two seniors who play the same position, but their families do not have the money that the freshman family has.

They also were putting seniors and juniors on the junior varsity team and putting players that should have been on junior varsity on the varsity team because the parents wanted their boys to get scholarships to college sports teams. I played football all four years of high school. I played in one game exactly nine minutes forty-five seconds on my senior year. I played a defensive back during that time. I was able to get ten tackles for losses during that one game time. I was told I was not very good at football by some of the players on my team. I had more single tackles that game than any of the other members of the whole team in that game.

I did letter in football, basketball, track, library club, and choir. I went to the state science fair two times and got an outstanding superior rating both times. I also went to the state music contest and got and outstanding and a superior rating. I also went to the state history fair and got an honorable mention, which was later changed to an outstanding ratting.

I attended Albia High School for all four years of my high school experience. Like I said before, we lived only a block away. I could cut through our neighbor's backyard and be there in about two minutes. We did not have fences back then. One day while I was at school, some of the wise guys came up to me and told me I needed to quit the football team. I asked them why, and they said that their girlfriends were admiring how hard I was playing but not getting to play in a game and they were going to go to the coach or school board. They wanted to see me get a chance also to play. They were trying to make it rough on me. I said I was not a quitter and if the coach wanted me to quit, to let him call me in and tell me to quit the team.

I continued to play for I believed that I could play as well as any as the other football players on the team, and I even asked the coach how I was doing, and he said, "Do not let the other players bother you. They are just jealous because their girlfriends are looking at you not them." He said, "Keep up the good work and you will letter for sure in football." I did play in a game my senior year and made ten tackles myself for losses, and you should have heard the crowd yell for joy. The coach was jumping up and down, and the others on the team just could not believe it. I even tackled the other team back in their own end zone one time, giving us two points, which gave us the game that night. I was carried off the field by the team.

I also ran track, the low huddles, and the half mile relay and the mile run. The hurdle race was 120 yards long. I was not the greatest doing that event even though I tried. I remember one time we had a track meet right after school. I was dizzy, and the hurdles was my first event. I got down in my stance, and when the gun went off, I fell and hit the ground. I got up and started running and run right into the first hurdle falling over it. I got up, and I kept going, doing the same thing with all the hurdles till I crossed the finish line, then I collapsed on the ground. Believe it or not, I got an honorable mention ribbon just for finishing the race in the condition I was in. I was real dizzy and could not see clear at all. I did not run any of the other events that day for I was in too much pain.

There was still times of hostility from the guys on the sports teams because of what I had been doing or the recognition I was getting. One Saturday, I was riding my bicycle home from work. I worked at a produce and feed store on Saturday grading eggs and collecting eggs and milk from farmers in the country area. The boss and I would go out and pick up eggs and milk and deliver feed all over a fifty-mile radius from the work site and back.

Well, back to what I was talking about. I was just about three to four blocks from my home when a pick-up truck carrying four boys (I knew the driver and the passengers in the truck but will not mention names because of criminal charges that could have been brought against them) came racing down the street speeding. They saw me along the side of the road on my bicycle, and the driver turned his truck in to my direction and hit me and my bicycle so hard that it knocked me off my bicycle and threw me so hard I went up on some person's porch against their door.

The truck took off so fast you would think they thought they killed me or something. They did not wait around to see if I was alright or anything. The people from the house came to the door and seen me and came out to check on me, and they called the police. They also called my mother and told her what happened and that I would be going to the hospital. They also called an ambulance.

I went to the hospital and was placed in the hospital for a week for possible fractured ribs and bruises all over my body and a bad left leg pain where the truck hit me. X-ray were taken and revealed that I did have several fractures on some ribs, a left leg and right AC separation of my R shoulder. They were able to put it back in place. I had several bruises all over. Other than that, I seem to appear to be okay, just upset at what had happen to me because of those foolish boys that always want to have their way just because they think they are big shots in school. My bicycle was destroyed and could not be fixed.

I had several visitors from school come to see me and try to find out if I was going to press charges against the boys from the school. Some of the visitors were the girlfriends of the boys that were in the truck. The coach came to see me, and he said he would take care of the problem and I would be well taken care of and watched over by the ones who he think is causing the problems. I did not have any more problems after that. After I got out of the hospital, I found out that a new bicycle had been delivered to my house for me. I had friends all over the place helping me out from then on in school. My grades improved, and I started liking school a whole lot more and getting involved in a lot more activities.

I joined the library club and worked in the library for two years. I learned the Dewey Decimal System and other interesting thing about the library system of books. I checked books in and out for students and put them back to their original position when they were returned. I even mended books that were torn or damaged when they were returned. Some people may say that this job was for a girl, but there was a lot of hard and heavy work, hauling a lot of books around and putting them away in the proper place. There were several guys in the library club, and I was proud of every one of them. Several of them were also on the sports teams alongside with me.

I also sang in the high school choir as a base tenor. We had a large group of singers and several were males. It sounded pretty good when we all got together to put on a concert for the school. We did not all get to practice together. We had small groups working together. When we had a concert or a contest, then we would all come together as one body. We had one of the best choirs in the state. We were always getting real high marks for our abilities. Our solos were also getting outstanding high superior ratings. I got two high outstanding superior ratings for two solos. I sang "Precious Lord" and "How Great Thou Art." I still cry when I hear someone singing these songs.

I graduated in 1967 of a class of 209 students. I really do not know for sure if I was in the top 10 percent, but I think I made it in the top 15 percent. I had a B+ to an A- average and was happy to get it. I believe with what I had to go through my life, I think even from kindergarten, I had to prove myself the next year that I was as good as the others, and I did. I got put back up with my peer group and stayed up with them even though I had to struggle with fights and bangs and bruises. I proved to them I could do and was as good as they were. I even went to the hospital for them to prove I was as good as they were, but I made it through to graduation, and I did not quit.

I lived up to our school motto, "Strong in will to strive, to seek, and not to yield." "A quitter never wins, and a winner never quits." That was me. I was who I was. I never quit, and I hope I became the winner.

THANK YOU, MR. WILSON. Wherever you are today, I want you to know that I owe it all to you for you were my inspiration.

Section 4: Different Schools Attended

As I stated from my first chapter, I attended several different schools. They all had varying degrees of charm and differences from kindergarten in Iowa to Lincoln Elementary in Oskaloosa, Iowa. There was not too much of a change. Then came CR Anderson Elementary and middle school in Helena, Montana. That was a shell shocker, quite different from what one would expect from a school. It was located in the Rocky Mountains. The weather seemed dusty and dry to me then would change to a cooler with more windy-type weather.

We had to ride a bus fifteen to twenty miles to start with to go to school into town. I did get used to it and started liking it. When we moved to town in Helena, Montana, we still went to the same school, so nothing changed till we decided to move again, which we did. Then we moved back to Eddyville, Iowa where I was in Eddyville Middle School for about a few months. It was a small country-type school, and things were slow and easy-going, and I had no problems while I was there. I did what I was told and went home to our farmhouse in the country.

We then move to Albia, Iowa, where I spent the next four years of my high school years. They were not easy for me, but I grew up and learned how to be a man and stand on my own two feet and not be a quitter. I had to make a lot of decisions while I was in high school that would help me be who I would be the rest of my life. I had to learn how to not be afraid of what laid around the next corner. I had to be prepared to take on the challenges what-ever they were. I didn't know what was going to happen to me or where I was going in life, but I knew that I would always have one person I could count on, helping me out when I needed it. I could call on the Lord to help me and give me the guidance I needed to make it through the difficult situations if I just trust in his guidance. Like our motto told us that I will never forget, "Strong in will to strive to seek and not to yield," and "A quitter never wins, and a winner never quits."

Here is a picture, of me when I graduated from high school. I was not the greatest looker toward the girls to me. I did stay neat and clean and did not look like a bum. A lot of the girls thought I was cute and rather handsome! I thought there were several better-looking guys in our class in school in my opinion. The girls just did not seem to be chasing me or getting dreamy eyed over me like they did over other guys.

I did have my eye on one girl that was very attractive and made my heart seem to flutter when she walked by me. I, Robert, could never tell her that because other guys seemed to be able to talk to her and make conversations with her so much easier. I really was just too shy around girls. Today I have no problem. I can hold long conversations with that girl. It is just so strange how over the years I realized that I found out that she wanted me also to talk to her just like the other guys back in high school did. She was a real decent girl and was willing to talk anytime I needed or wanted to talk to her, and I just did not know it. All I really had to do is ask her for help, and she would have helped me.

This is me my high school graduation getting my diploma for graduating from high school. I, Robert, graduated with a B+ to A- average. I was shocked. I was in the top 11 percent of the class. A lot of the students were surprised also, and they were happy for me because they always thought I appeared that I was just and average Joe and really did not mean too much to the school. When they found out that I achieved a position, which was in the top 11 percent of the class, the upper classmates started taking notice of me.

I had a lot of them saying they were sorry for treating me as they did. They came to me and said, "You proved to us that you were as smart as we were, and you did more than we did because you stood up to us all and said you would not quit when we thought you were beaten. You rose back up and continued and became a winner. We are proud of you."

I do also have a picture of my mother and I when I got my diploma.

This was just a picture of my graduation from high school in Albia, Iowa. I will never forget those days. It brings back a lot of fond memories. But now I am heading to a new future and new things to do. We shall see how I will handle the challenge of the future.

This was my mother and I at my graduation, and she was really proud of me and what I had accomplished. She thought the choices I made for the future were all good and would take me along in a good direction. I had decided to go into the medical field. I did discussed the idea with my family first and decided since I had been notified that I was being drafted, I just might as well enlist into the army after I do graduate for it does not look like my college deferment is going to be in time from avoiding the draft. So I decided to make plans to enlist and take the test to get into the medical field in the service.

I commenced to the testing site and took a series of test in Des Moines, Iowa, called entrance exams and placement test to see if I, Robert, qualified to get into the medical field. I passed in flying colors with a 149 score. They told me I, Robert, could get into almost any field I wanted. I, Robert, told them I wanted to be a male nurse to start with. They told me I could or would start out as a 91B then go to 91C LPN School when I returned from Vietnam. They told me the reason why I could not get into the higher school program right now was because of the war that is going on in Vietnam. They are needing replacements. After I return, I could continue my education to the next level. I was told I then could be tested to see if I qualified for PA School Program down the road if I stayed in the service.

It sounded good to me. It looked like all I had to do is return from Vietnam, and my education would by waiting on me to me to just go while being in the service. It was also being paid for by the army. That sounded like a deal I could not pass up at that time, plus they were going to give me an enlistment bonus to be sent home for safe keeping of $20,000. On May 24, 1967 I signed the papers to enlist into the United States Army. This was twelve days after I graduated from high school from Albia, Iowa, 1967.

This is the girl I took to the High School Prom. I also worked on her dad's farm until I had to go to the bus station to leave for the Army. I enjoyed the summer very much. I got sunburned quite a bit on my back. Sue, to protect her name, put lanoline shaving cream on my back three times a day to ease up the burn. It really helped because in a very few days, it did not hurt at all. I never will forget that summer and the love and friendship we shared. I really hated for it to end the way it did. She was such a loving person. I will always cherish her for her kindness toward me. Her dad taught me how to drive a tractor and how to plow a field. I even helped paint his barn deep red trimmed in white. It looked pretty good when we were done with it. I stayed with them till June 4, 1967. At such time, I went home and left for the bus station three days later.

CHAPTER 2

Letter from US Army Headquarters

Section 1: Letter of Intent to Be Inducted into the United States Army May 24, 1967

When I graduated from high school, I had been waiting for a college deferment to Lafayette University for entrance into their medical training course to become a doctor. I had not heard a word by graduation, but I did receive a letter right on graduation day from our friendly United States Army letting me know that I was number one on the draft notification board of Iowa. I had twenty-four hours to enlist into the service or be drafted into the army. I studied the odds of receiving my deferment to go to college, and it was not good. I decided to join the Army and go into medical field as a 91B.

Since I had a couple of months, I decided to work for a while to get my mind off the army and everything else I was leaving behind. I did not know what to do with myself, and I was really getting uneasy about leaving all my family and friends behind. I took long walks to ease my mind and to try

38

and relax, but it was hard. I had a girlfriend and told her I would write her as often as I could. I did not really know if she would write me. I was just wishing. She would. I do not know if there were any more people from our town called up to duty. I would not know till the day I got on the bus for Des Moines Recruiting station.

I talked to our bishop or branch president of our church about my life and what I was about to do. I was scared about going off to a battle zone for the fear of not returning. He told me that God was not a mean God and sent people to their death without a good reason. He would protect me and allow me to grow up to be a man. He would be there with me when I needed his help. It would be like a mission going to Vietnam. I could do the Lord's work for him right where it was needed most, and he would guide me through. So I decided this was going to be my mission call for the church, and I would be protected and guided by the Lord's hand if I obeyed his commandments. Even if I met with adversity, I would ask the Lord for his guidance.

Section 2: Worked One Month on Road Construction (Glover) Before Entering Service

I started working for Glover Construction Company. It was a road construction outfit that fixed roads that had a lot of potholes and bad road. I first worked leveling the road wires on the sides of the road so the paving machine would lay down and even amount of asphalt on the highway. I also worked as a road guard, stopping cars and trucks at a certain point as other vehicles were coming through from the other side. It was a very hot and tiring job. The money was good. I was able to save $2300 for my mother in the month I worked. I told her it was a gift to her for all the love and things she had done for me. She was to spend it on whatever she wanted and not worry about paying it back. She was happy about getting something from one of her children unconditionally. I added a $100 to the amount just before I left, and she went out and got a twenty-four-thousand-dollar savings bond and said she was going to save it till I returned home.

The work that I did was hard work, and it did take my mind off of leaving so soon. We worked in Northwest Iowa around Mason City. They had a lot of bad roads due to the winter weather they had. The time passed by rather quickly, and I had to return home to get ready to go on my trip to the recruiting station. I was told I could work my way up and go to school while in the service and get a degree in nursing, which I wanted anyway. I was told I was prone to go to a field unit as an infantry medic but could get assigned to a hospital unit in the States first. But as luck would have it, my basic training was at Fort Polk, Louisiana. I did not start basic training till July 10, 1967. They gave me a couple of months to get my paperwork in order and my pay in order of who was going to maintain it while I was in Vietnam. I just finished my two-month preparation and was ready to go to the bus station.

Section 3: Waiting at Bus Stop in Albia, Iowa, to Go to Induction Station in Des Moines, Iowa

The bus stop in Albia, Iowa, was located at the edge of the square uptown. I figured I would have to stand there all alone to get on the bus, but I was surprised. It seemed that the whole town knew I, was leaving, and they came out to send me off. My friends from high school were there, and the staff, the principal, and my counselors were there. Other people were getting on the bus also. My whole family was there to send me off. There was no one else going into the service from our town but me. It made me feel warm all over having this much attention given me by so many people. They all thanked me for being loyal enough to serve our country in time of war. And said that they would pray for my safe return and would have a reunion when I came home. Even the boys that put me in the hospital a few years earlier were there and apologized and told me I would come home a decorated hero. I thanked them and said I pray that they will be alright and make it through college. I said I will get there and get my degree. I said I would miss all of them very much and would make Albia proud of me.

Section 4: Bus Trip to Des Moines then to Fort Polk, Louisiana

After saying all my goodbye, I got on the bus, and we were off to Des Moines to the induction station where I had a physical and found myself fit for duty. I was given some shots and given some army clothing and gear with a duffle bag full of stuff. It seemed like I was on an assembly line. Next, I headed for the barber shop for a haircut, not for a normal haircut but a buzz. That is where they cut it all off, leaving you with just a short stubble. Least it was cool because it was hot outside around 86 degrees. We were in Des Moines about three to five hours, then we were loaded back on a bus and taken to Fort Polk, Louisiana, Tiger Land Basic Training Area. I was supposed to be going to Fort Leonard Wood, Missouri. Somehow my orders got changed at the last minute. We were on our way to Fort Polk, and I had been told that anyone who goes there is going to war for it is called Little Vietnam. They train as if you are in the front lines in the battle front. There is a basic training and an advance training there, and you must go through both before you can go to your specialized advanced training course.

Section 5: Arrival at Tiger Land Basic Training at Fort Polk, Louisiana, South Fort

When our bus arrived at Fort Polk, we were greeted by several drill sergeants. They started yelling at us to line up in a formation and started giving us instructions the moment we got off the bus. They tried to place us in certain squads and platoons. It was a hassle, but it was finally done, and I was assigned to a squad, platoon, and company. I found out since I was an Eagle Scout I was automatically made a PFC and a squad leader. I jumped two strips all at once.

Basic training had a lot of different things to learn to do. It would be too hard to name them all. I believe the hardest was low crawling under a barbed wire set up for about 120 yards plus in the sloppy mud with live fire over your head. You only had so much time to do it in or the firing would get lower to you. I learned to low craw through it pretty good and fast. There was also the grenade range where we had to engage a target then pull a pin on a grenade and throw it a certain way as to put it into a type of bunker entrench-ment. I witnessed many explode before they went into the entrenchment.

The riffle range was also not the easiest thing to do. There were many positions they had us firing an M14 and an M16 from and an M30 machine gun, and a 45 caliber hand gun from the various positions they wanted us in. I was able to get an expert badge in all except the grenade throw, and I got an outstanding marksman in it. We had to climb tall ropes and pole fences and high rope ladders and come down the other side to another object to maneuver around. We had to do a lot of running and marching with heavy ruck sacks on our backs. When I say marches, I mean long marches of fifty to a hundred miles long at times. We would live off the land at time, eating berries and drinking water we had to decontaminate ourselves with our chlorination kits. We learned what was eatable in the woods and what was not. It helped a lot to make sure we had our backpack full of small eatable things so we could survive for a while if we ever got lost from our unit or became missing in action.

One thing I did not have to do while I was in basic training was pull kitchen police duty. I was made a squad leader, so I got out of KP duty. The soldiers that did kitchen police duty told me they had to peel thousands of potatoes and scrub pot and pans all day and clean the mess hall three times each day they had the duty. They also had other duties, but I will not go into it.

Basic training was eight weeks long, but after it was over, a person felt like he had been there for a year. We were so tired and wanted to go on leave. There was no real time to take a leave because we all were being transferred to the second training site for Tiger Land Basic 2 at North Fort. This was the real deal. We are going to train as if we are in the jungles of Vietnam. We have the job to clean this company area first. We will go to the new company Monday. They want this place clean as a white glove, as the Army would say.

After we passed inspection, we were on our way to North Fort. We got in formation with our rucksacks and our rifles and our steel post on our heads. We began a marching to North Fort, which was thirty-two miles away. It did not take to long for us to march that distance. When we arrived, it was, in my opinion, secluded or hidden in a deep jungle-type forest. I could not see hardly anything that looked like a building or a tent. It was going to be interesting how this place was set up from where the entrance of the encampment was located, which was about five miles from the actual training center.

Section 6: Second North Tiger Land Advanced Training at North Fort

The following Monday, we were all transferred to North Fort for Advanced Tiger Land Training. This place was known as Little Vietnam. Why? I did not know, but I would soon find out. We went through the same routine: getting us placed in a squad, platoon, and company. I, again, was made a squad leader and promoted to Specialist Four acting. I was told I would be promoted to SP 4 for real when I got to my AIT (Advanced Individual Training) unit.

I gained another strip, and I had not even got out of basic training yet. I had a lot of responsibility placed on me. Though that was going to take some doing to preform, I assured myself I would do it. Advanced basic training was twelve weeks long and more intense than basic ever was. It was like we were in the middle of a battlefield and we were being pursued by the enemy this time. We had to use our minds and our skills we learned in basic training to outwit the enemy and become the victors.

We learned a lot more strategies and ways of doing things that would help defeat the enemy in battle. We learned how to live in the dark and move around using equipment to see in the dark. We learned how to hide ourselves during the day so it would be hard for the enemy to see us. Depending on our jobs, we learned how to keep one eye watching the surrounding area for snippers or enemy's soldiers in the areas or buildup of crowds. We learned about bombs and land mines and how they might be buried in the ground to be set off. We also learned how to defuse explosive devices and how to set up a perimeter of explosive devices for protecting our post.

We would have fake raids on our post at night by the enemy then an alarm would go off, and we would have to go to the perimeter line at various positions, and we would have a mad minute where we would shoot our weapons off and get rid of all our old ammunition. We would be shooting at targets that were moving around in the dark about seventy-five yards away. This was the enemy outrunning around the post trying to get in. They would be firing back, so we had to be in trenches for protection. It made it feel like a real live firefight was taking place. Some people got hurt not doing what they were told to do.

We had to climb wooden walls that were high and then come down on a rope on the other side and continue running across logs places in our path. It was like an obstacle course—long and hard to do. We also still had to take long marches day or night trying to get from point A to point B in a certain length of time. If we did not meet the time, we would have to do it again till we did meet the time limit. The time would be shortened each time. So we had to be on our toes and in hurry up mode all the time. To say the least, it was not easy.

We had to grow up and become men—well-defined men working as a team or it could cost us our lives. If someone got hurt, we helped him, and we moved on and trained another to take the place of the injured solider. We had a mission, and we could not wait for one person to get well before we went on. It sounded cruel, but that is how war is. The mission comes first. It did really seemed like the war movies you see on TV with all the blood and guts being played out as if it was a real-life situation, and we had to react or be injured in the process. This was for real. We were training for war, no if and or buts. We do it or pay the price.

We went through twelve weeks of drills and classes. We spent many nights in discussion groups, talking about the enemy and just who the enemy was. Little children were in the group of possible enemies because they plant mines in the road right outside your post. They will walk up to you with a grenade in their hand with the pin pulled and hand it to you, letting it roll out of their hands. Within three seconds, it will explode. They will throw grenades into trucks with GI's in them. You cannot really trust anyone. You had to keep your eyes open and your ears listening to what was going on around you all the times.

We had barracks inspection. It seemed like every other day. The drill sergeants checked us for shaving, haircuts, how we made our beds, how we keep the floors, the Latrines, and how we shined our shoes and how we keep and pressed and cleaned our clothes. Everything had to be just so neat and tidy or we got in trouble and ended up on KP duty. We had to keep enough money to get a haircut every week. We polished our boots every night. They wanted a spit shin on them. We had two pair of boots, so if one pair got muddy and wet, it could dry over-night, and we could polish them in the morning. I got good at taking care of my shoes. They never complained about my shoes. Our clothes were sent to the cleaners, so they always came back pressed and clean. Our footlockers were kept in an orderly fashion with everything in a certain place folded neatly.

We were allowed to go on pass two times for the weekend while we were as Fort Polk, Louisiana, Advance Basic. I went to church both time and met a very nice family from Rose Pine. They had a daughter about my age, who was very beautiful with red hair. She promised to write to me when I

00088012851

went to Vietnam. I said I would write to her. Her name was Judy (for her protection and privacy, I will not reveal her true name.) The family had me over for Sunday dinner on both my passes. I really got to caring for their family, and I wrote home and told my mother about them. Finally, the twelve weeks were over, and now I could go to my real advanced individual training. I was going to Fort Sam Houston in San Antonio, Texas. I was going to the 91B Medical Specialist Combat Medic School. It was also a twelve-week medical training course in emergency medicine and combat medicine. It also had a one-week field hospitalization training set up in the course where we would go to the field and set up and operate a field and a division clearing station hospital staging area.

CHAPTER 3
Advanced Individual Training

As I said, I was transferred to San Antonio, Texas, for medical 91B Medical Specialist Combat Medic School. It was also a twelve-week course of combat medicine. We went through the same routine of being assigned to a squad, platoon, and company. This time I had the shock of my life given to me. I was promoted to the Specialist 4th class or SP4 like they told me I would be in Fort Polk, Louisiana. I must be doing something right to be getting promoted like I was. I was also made a squad leader again.

We had to go through a lot of classes this time and be tested from each class. We had classed on bandages and splinting, to casting, dressing head wounds, to chest and lung wounds, to leg and arm amputations. There was just so much to learn in twelve weeks. It was impossible to be 100 percent accurate all the time. On top of all the class work, we had field drills where we went out in the field and had mass casualty exercises. We also learned how to medivac patients to a clearing station hospital or a field hospital or an aid station for further treatment. We learned how to carry patients on a litter and load them in a helicopter or ambulance or truck ambulance or across a jeep or in a truck bed.

We learned how to deliver a baby and get transportation by medivac or ambulance to the nearby town for further evaluation. We learned how to take care of snake bites, anaphylactic shock, and bee sting. There is just so much stuff that was taught. It was mind blowing. It was interesting as all get out. I enjoyed every minute of it. I did not know if I would ever use any of or all of it, but I would want to be prepared.

We went back to the classroom as if we were working in the hospital and learned how to take care of patients in beds, giving baths, putting in catheters, changing dressings, changing linen with the patient in bed. We also learned how to start IVs and take blood if needed. We learned to take temperature, pulse, and respiration and blood pressure on every patient we had. We all had a turn in the emergency room of the hospital. There we learned of all the bad things that can happen to someone on the outside you do not always hear about: over dosses, shooting, car crashes, falls, heart attacks, strokes, beatings, just everything comes through the emergency room door. You, as medical personnel, need to be ready to take care of them the best way you can.

It is no wonder the training is so long and so much given to you at one time. There is so much to learn. There is no time for slacking off on your job. The last week of training we are back out in the field again, learning emergency surgery like suturing wounds and also possible watching a tracheostomy being performed in case that we may have to do it someday. We also learned how to set up a field and a division clearing station hospital and maintain it under field conditions and operations. This was the end of our medical training.

Section 2: A Combat Medical Specialist Faces War with Many Challenges Ahead to Perform

We have finished our training, and we are ready to be sent to Vietnam. We are to have a graduation ceremony today at 10:00 a.m. I know my parents came from Iowa to be at the graduation. We were to get a thirty-day leave before shipping out to Vietnam. That does not always happen I found out. We had a good ceremony, but something did not seem right toward the end of it.

The captain of the ceremony stood up and called attention to the troops, which in turn we all stood up. He then announced that as further notice, all leaves were cancelled. And then called for the guards to come in. They came in with rifles and field gear on as if they were going to take us somewhere. The captain announced to the parents and audience that all the companies that were on the stage for graduation were being escorted to Travis Air Force Base, Washington, for immediate deployment to the Republic of Vietnam and all leaves were canceled.

He said all our bags are packed and on the cattle truck. We do not have to get nothing! And that we would be headed down the highway within minutes. We did not even get a chance to say goodbye to our family that came to see us and take us home on leave. I am sure they were quite upset. I am sure they explained the situation to all the audience so they would not be so worried and upset. We were then marched out of the auditorium right into a cattle truck with the guards.

SURPRISE, I AM STILL HERE,
TO TELL MY STORY, AFTER MANY YEARS

The training was over, and now we were about to take a long journey to a far country where we will meet up with other soldiers who have been fighting a war with an enemy that is well-trained in warfare. They want to win as much as you want to stop them from winning. Before I forget, what happens when I go to Vietnam, I would or we had one more trip to the woods to set up a clearing hospital and aid station. We stocked it with what we thought we would need if we were out in the jungles. We could be stationed in a place like this in the very near future, so we wanted to have what we needed to take care of patients, and to be able to medivac them to the next staging area they needed to go, so they would get the best care they would get. I only hope I learned enough so I can do the best job I know how and hopefully help several soldiers make it back home that might not have made it if I had not helped them. We were official combat medics and prepared to go fight for the Freedom for the United States and to help South Vietnam.

This is a couple of poems I wrote while on the way over to the Republic of Vietnam to my girlfriend I left behind at Fort Polk, Louisiana.

ETERNITY BY A SOLDIER

THE READER—THEE

THE POET—ME

THE SUBJECT—WE

THE CRITIC—HE

A TENNIS SHOE—THEE

A JUNGLE—BOOTED ME

THEN A GLOWING—THEE

BESIDE A PROUD—ME

ONE ETERNAL—WE

A CARING—HE

NOW SCHOOL—FOR THEE

AND WAR—FOR ME

A FOOTLOOSE—WE   A YEAR—BEFORE WE
A GUIDING—HE   A—WATCHING HE

SCHOOL—THEE   A PROBLEM—FOR THEE
CHINA SEA—ME   NO PROBLEM—FOR ME
A CLOSER—HE   AND A HELPING HE
APARTMENT—FOR THEE   A PRAYER FOR—THEE

A HOOCH—FOR ME   A PRAYER—FOR ME
A HOUSE—FOR WE   A KNEELING—WE
BUILT—UNTO HE   AN ANSWERING—HE

THE SECOND POEM IS CALLED "SUNDAY." I AM NOT
THE AUTHOR, BUT IT IS HOW I FELT THAT DAY.

Sunday… It is hard to believe it can be so quiet
After such a noisy Saturday night

There were so many words I wanted to say last night
Words I am afraid of like tomorrow, and together, and love.
If I say I love you,
I want it to mean more than I love peanut butter or James
    Bond movies,
I want it to mean I am letting go for always,
That I will not turn back
I have never used the word before I've been afraid. Once you
    say you love somebody, you can' take it back, but let
    us not talk about love, let us talk about dogs or sum-
    mertime, Or we can read the funny papers out loud.
    Or we can go to the zoo or just stay here like we are.
    Come out along the trees with me, you never knew my

middle name, I never told you that. Do you know I can stand on my hands almost! There is probably a mole somewhere down your back that escaped my eyes in the darkness. We need to know it all. Everything that brought us into each other's eyes and why. All those mysteries that we save for no one. We can give to one another where did the night go, already it is Sunday. I Loved You. And I have to Go.

LOVE
Love Is Like A Pot Of Gold,
Hard To Get And Hard To Hold.
Of All The Girls I Ever Met,
You're The One I Can Not Forget
.

Roses love sunshine,
Violets love dew.
The angels in heaven,
Know I love you.

CHAPTER 4

Back across the US to Start Over to Get Orders for Overseas Duty

As I said, we were all standing on stage at our graduation ceremony. Most of us were going to go home on a thirty-day leave before our next assignment. We had not gotten an assignment yet. Then a group of fully dressed military police came marching in with fully loaded M16s weapons surrounding our company and the people on the stage. A spokesman went to the podium and announced that the following company of soldiers have had their leaves revoked and they will be on direct orders to be sent to Travis Air Force Base in the state of Washington. They then will be sent to the Republic of Vietnam.

Our parents in the audience were in a state of disbelief, but it was true. We did not even get to say goodbye. We were marched straight from the stage right into a large truck like a cattle truck with seats. The military police got on the truck or trucks with us, and we found out that our clothing and baggage were already loaded. We headed straight out to the interstate, heading for Travis Air Force Base. The trucks had two latrines located in a couple areas on the trucks.

The only time we stopped was for the driver to get gas and oil for the truck. We were not allowed to get off the truck. It took us a couple of days to get there, but we did get there. When we unloaded, we were marched to a holding area till we got our orders for Vietnam, and then we were divided into different groups. I guess that was because we were going to different areas of Vietnam. We went back to the holding area and was given a flight number and seat number and was told to stay in the holding area till our names and flights and seat numbers were called. It could be in hours or even a few days before we got on the plane. In my case it was, the next day before I got on the plane to head for Viet Nam

Section 2: Plane Ride to the Republic of South Vietnam

We got to Travis Air Force Base in the mid-afternoon of February 1968. It was cold outside, and we all hurried into the building where we knew it would be warm. We were shocked by the warm welcome we got when we did enter the building. People were standing in line to shake our hands and tell us that they cared about us and what we were about to do. It made me feel good that someone cared that we were leaving to war to fight for their freedom.

We were all escorted down the hall and to the right. We ended up at the back of the terminal in the corner. It appeared like a cargo area. After further investigation, it was a cargo staging area for the C130 cargo planes of the US Air Force and Army. As I said before, we were separated and went to a holding area where we had to get a flight number and a seat number. We were then taken back to the holding area where we waited for our seat number to be called out. When we got our call, we then were loaded on two or three of the C130s, and the guards were loaded right on behind us for they were going to Vietnam also. We were all in the air in about twenty-four hours with the taxing down the runaway.

The flight took thirty-seven to forty-one hours to get to Vietnam. We sat in a type of cargo seat, not like a regular airplane seat. It was made from parachute material tied together in a certain way. It was not comfortable. We also had to put on a parachute and strap it to our back in case of emergency because we were going over the ocean. If the plane should have problems, we would be prepared for any emergency. We still did not have our orders as to where we were going to be stationed. We would not know till we got to Vietnam staging area. I sat there doing a lot of thinking and praying and decided I would not tell mom or my stepdad where I really was going to be stationed because I did not want them to have to worry about me all the time. I will tell them I am I got stationed in a hospital unit out of danger. I was hoping I would be sent to a place like that anyway.

We are now 41,000 feet from the ground and over the Pacific Ocean. The cloud layer is below us, so it is clear up this high right now. When it got dark out, we should be able to see the stars well. I might be asleep and miss the beauty of the sky and the great northern lights that shine forth in this part of the world. Up here, even with the engines of the plane running, it still appeared quiet and still. I think everyone was in their own little world. I had been thinking a lot about home and a lot about where I would be going for the next thirteen months. I hoped it would go by quickly so we all could go home together.

I found out that there are a few soldiers on the plane that only would be there for five months. That is how much time they have left in the service. They just gave us a sack lunch from McDonalds to eat. Least they thought of something good to eat for the trip. We even got a can of soda or a milk shake and fries. It was even hard to eat up here because my stomach was upset already. It is because I was afraid of being so high up, and I was also home sick for my family already. Thirty-seven to forty-one hours is sure a longtime riding in this seat as uncomfortable as it was. There were three to four potty rooms at different locations in the plane for us to use. I did use them several times just to move around.

I finally got to see the great northern lights a little. It was beautiful from up there in the sky. The stars were bright and made the sky shine forever. We finally made our descent into the Me Kong Delta Air Force Base area. As we were touching down, we could hear in a distance some incoming fire. As we got closer to the terminal, we had a mortar round shot at our plane and hit just under a wing. It scared us all. We were told as we get off the plane to run to the terminal fast. We had another mortar round come in, and this time it did hit just beside the wing and under the plane, on the plane's right side about where I would have been sitting just above the wing and to the right first scat closest to the window. The terminal was like a bunker of sandbags made into a large building and hallways and other rooms off the side of it. There were trucks all over the place to take soldiers where they were to go when they got their orders.

CHAPTER 5

Landing in the Mekong Delta of South Vietnam

I stayed at the Me Kong Delta Air Force Base area overnight and got my orders the next day. They told me they were subject to change. For now, I was being assigned to D Company Nineteenth Combat Engineer Battalion. It was located at a place called LZ Debbie about 150 or so miles north of where we were right now, along the mountainous region.

The engineer's job was to mine sweep eighty or so miles of road per day and make sure the road stayed clear of mines so traffic could use the road. They also were to defuse any mines or bombs planted in the road or mountains that the infantry patrols used. I will get into some of the situation of mines later, but first, let me get to the company.

It was not an easy ride to the company. Remember in basic training when I said they told us not to trust even the little kids. They were right. As we loaded into the back of a truck the ones going to where I was going, the truck had to go through this small town or village. A little girl came up to the truck and threw a live grenade into the back of it. We all scrambled to jump out. We had four casualties right off the bat for me to take care of. They all had to go to the hospital for surgery. Two would be returning home with an amputee.

That woke me up right fast that this place was not going to be a picnic. We had to stop three times because some of the trucks had hit gunfire or hit a land mine and taken on casualties. I am lucky they gave me an aid bag at the deployment site. I took care of thirteen patients before I got to my company. Oh yes, we also had to stop because a mama-san (woman) fell in front of one of the trucks. I checked her out and then delivered a six-pound-eight-ounces baby boy. We got transportation to a local doctor (called a boxy) for her, and we were on our way again.

It was a busy but learning day for me, I must say in the least. I certainly was not expecting to see so much action on my first day on the job and on the way to my company where I would spend the next year of my life. It looked like I was in for a very busy year with a lot of things to do and learn. Lord, please help me do my best the time I have over here in Vietnam.

SURPRISE, I AM STILL HERE,
TO TELL MY STORY, AFTER MANY YEARS

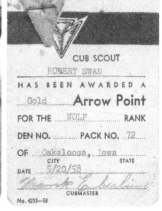

CUB SCOUT

ROBERT SWAN

HAS BEEN AWARDED A

Gold **Arrow Point**

FOR THE .....WOLF..... RANK

DEN NO. .... PACK NO. .72....

OF ..Oskaloosa, Iowa..........
     CITY   STATE

DATE 5/20/58

CUBMASTER

No. 4233—58

CHAPTER 6

Company Nineteenth Combat Engineer Battalion

Camp LZ Debbie was a large encampment up the side of a mountain about a mile up. It was made of all sandbags and wood with some metal roofing layered with more sandbags on top of it. The commanding officer greeted us and introduced his senior officers. He then gave one of his officers the duty to take the new soldiers that just arrived on a tour of the compound. So we were given a brief description of the entire company area and layout of the company headquarters and mess hall and sleeping quarters and medical aid station, company latrines, and motor pool.

We were taken and given a meal in the mess hall of water buffalo that was given to the company by a local farmer. We also had beans and a salad that looked a week old and some bread and a drink of water, milk or coffee or tea. It was not much, but it was something to eat. The food was not the greatest ever around here. Our C rations we took to the field seemed to have more flavor than the so-called home-cooked meals we ate in this mess hall. Like I said, there was a mess hall that was a large GP medium tent encased in sandbags and held up with wooden poles and doors with heavy-duty screens on them. It had picnic tables for tables and seats. This is where they ate and had all their company meetings.

They had a commanding office and clerk's office all in one encased in sandbags and lined with wood and metal like the other enclosures. The sleeping quarters were made of half metal tubes about 150 feet long or more with sandbags encasing them quite thick so they would withstand up to a big motor blast upon it. There were ten latrines with four stool fixtures each. It made it feel a little more homey. There were ten four-man shower stalls in an encased building-type structure of sandbags wood cement.

There was a motor pool and vehicles with a garage encased in sandbags and wood. It had all the things needed to work on a vehicle and more. There were twelve sleeping quarters, but they were not the same size. Some were for officers, and some for enlisted. The enlisted were broken up into job duty area of work. We had about 275 men in our company. There were also some smaller quarter made for the higher ranking officers and guests that that would come by every now and then. They were all encased in heavy sand-bags. There was a storage area and a garbage dump and a waste dump.

We also had a small artillery unit further up the moun-tain side, which consisted of eight total Quad 50s and eight total thirty-caliber machine guns mounted on jeeps. They also had four M80 tanks with a long tube mortar gun mounted on it. They were there to protect the mountain top from being invaded by the enemy and to go on the mine sweeps with the engineers during the day. They had four placements on top of the mountain with all the same things. They were kept busy at night because of incoming fire by snippers.

We had a berm line that went completely around our eight posts, and guards stood watch every night watching for any signs of trouble. If trouble was seen, the company was alerted, and everyone reported to the berm except for four medics. They went to the make-shift aid station in case they had wounded come in. Other medics went to the berm for help there and to bring casualties to the aid station.

The aid station was equipped with all the equipment needed to take care of the sick and injured soldier or soldiers. They also could call for medivac support. A helicopter was able to land right in the center of the compound or an ambulance could drive to pick up a patient when there was clearance and safe passage.

*****

This is another poem I wrote for all my friends back in high school in Albia, Iowa, graduating class of 1967

WHAT DO THEY MEAN TO ME!

FRIENDS THEY MEAN A HELL OF A LOT YOU MISS YOUR BUDDIES BACK HOME ON THE BLOCK
THE GIRLS BACK HOME YOU USED TO DATE
YOU MISS THEM TOO, BUT YOU'LL HAVE TO WAIT
AND COURSE YOUR MACHINE, YOUR GROVIE WHEELS
MISS THEM TOO? I KNOW HOW YOU FEEL
YOUR FAVORITE BAR WHERE YOU USED TO DRINK
BUT WAIT LET'S STOP AND THINK!!!

Yes, i think you'll all agree
That most of all we will miss
Our good old family!!

Section 2: First Firefight from Company Berm or Border

Our first firefight scared the ever living day light out of me. I was just about ready to go to bed the second day I was there, and I was tired from the long day's work we put in. We had to refill sandbags and put them on the aid station for more support. When it rains in Vietnam, the bags seem to fall apart, and the sand falls to the ground, and the bag loses its strength. So they needed to be replaced.

As I was saying, I was going to bed, and I heard an explosion in the compound that bought me to my feet in a hurry. I heard the alert siren go off. I headed for the aid station for I was the senior-ranking medic. There were all kinds of gunfire going on that I thought that we were being attacked by a lot of enemy. Later, I found out that it was just some sniper fire from a little berm about a half mile away. I was told they do it to agitate us at night and keep us up and tired, so we will make mistakes during the day locating the mines in the roads.

Speaking of that berm, one day not too long after I was there, I was sitting outside on a sandbag wall and drawing a picture. I was drawing a picture of a hillside about a quarter mile to a half mile away from our compound, and it looked funny. It appeared like black metal bars coming out every so often out through the ground. There were round looking objects every so often sticking out of the side of the berm and looked like pipes from the sun beaming down on them at times, maybe even gun barrels.

The hill was built up with what looked like holes in the ground ever so often too. The company commander came by and asked what I was doing, and I showed him my picture. He told me to wait right where I was at, and he went and got some field glasses to see where and what I was drawing. When he figured it out, he called for his company clerk and radio man. He then called in an air strike on the position that I drew. In a few minutes, an air strike hit the position he called in, and I found out that I had drew an underground tunnel berm with a gun port holes for snippers to shoot from. It ran for three to four miles long.

The company commander kept my picture and said I probably saved several people's lives with that picture. I was put in for a bronze star. He said they were setting up for a bigger attack on our compound and we beat them to the punch. The battalion commander came to or company to also present me with an army commendation medal for my being aware of my surroundings and looking out for the welfare of the entire company. He put my picture in his office at the battalion headquarters to show others what to look for right in their own backyard.

Section 3: First Few Mine Sweeps on Road on QL Eighty-One, A Quad 50 Was Our Support for the Eighty-Three Mile Trip

The first mine sweep of the road that I was involved in was about two weeks after I arrived on post LZ Debbie. They wanted me to get used to the place before I tackled a road job. They said it was quite hazardous to a person's health. It was quite scary at times. When the engineers found a mine in the road, they would disarm it or blow it in place so it would not blow up in someone's face or someone would step on it or vehicle would drive over it and blow it.

There was also the possibility of a firefight with the enemy while you were trying to do your job, and there could be a lot of injured soldiers. The company was not wrong for my first road trip was like walking down death row. We had to take care of several casualties. Three medics plus me, making four, took care of ten patients that had wounds that needed immediate attention. We had to medivac them to the battalion clearing hospital in North English. The reason was that the vehicle they were riding hit a mine buried in the road and we had not gone but three miles down the road of the eighty-one-mile trip. It was a long, long day.

Several days later when we went down the road, we found that the enemy had attacked a group of tanks drivers called the Midnight Riders, and they were shot up, and the tanks were torn apart and some disassembled and carried off or dragged off through the jungle. It seemed strange that the enemy could disassemble a complete tank and carry them off in just a few hours. We were there on site in about four to five hours from when they passed our post. The enemy must have had hundreds of people with them to pull a job off like that because they were four tanks they carried off and four they destroyed and tore apart.

They certainly knew what they were doing. They even planted some mines in the road for us to disarm. As we tried to get the dead and wounded soldiers out of the area that was from the convoy of tanks that were attacked. It was a big mess and a hard day and a very sad day to see so many deaths in one place. I know the mothers of these soldiers would be very sad to hear about their sons being attacked like this, and there was nothing that us, medics, could do but pull them from the ugly tank wreckage and medivac them too grave registration to be prepared to be sent home to their home sweet home of record.

It would be very hard to identify many of the soldiers for as bad as they were shot up and torn up from the mine explosions or grenade's thrown in on them. We just hoped and prayed that we got the right parts together with the right soldier.

Lord, forgive us if we failed in our job if we did not do it right. May the mother and fathers of these honorable soldiers who had fallen for our country know that they have not died in vain but were loyal to the end and deserve the highest respect one can give to a fallen comrade.

I, a medic in Vietnam, do salute your sons and your family for all your sacrifice and your care for this country. If I make it home from Vietnam, I will write a book and will include your sons' memories in the book for they were a true bunch of heroes in my life. I will always remember them. I do not know them by name, but I know they were the tank commanders of the Midnight Rider #4APC. APC Track Tank. APC stands for armored personnel carrier.

Section 4: Ambush on Road Several Casualties Medivac to Battalion Aid for Further Treatment

We had many trips down the road mine sweepings. There were several mines and booby traps found and blown in place. We also had several sniper fire incidents that happened that caused us to have several casualties of our own. On one occasion, I remember we were going down the road, and a jeep went into a big puddle of water I thought till it hit a mine, and it was then submerged in the water. We got incoming fire from the enemy, and we all did the best we could to get off the road and out of the way of the sniper fire.

Soldiers scattered behind rock that was along the side of the road as well as some bushes. The four soldiers in the jeep jump into the water, but two were wounded by the explosion from the mine. I managed to jump into the water and swim to the jeep and help pull the wounded soldiers out of the water and onto dry ground. One of the soldiers had an amputated left leg, which I applied a tourniquet to stop the bleeding and circulation. The other soldier had a gunshot wound to his left arm, which went all the way through. It just needed a good strong dressing. The other two in the jeep were able to swim out of the water and find cover bend the rocks.

If that was not enough, a mama-san (girl) came walking down the road who was pregnant. She walked right into the fire zone and got hit with gunfire. I ran out and pulled her out and off to the side and behind a large rock. I put a dressing on her leg where she had been shot and laid her down for she was about to give birth to her baby. She was scared, but we had a South Vietnam medic with us so he could calm her down.

I delivered her baby, and we were able to get transportation to a local doctor (boxy) in a village nearby for her to be taken. I was grateful for the help of the Vietnamese medic that was with me that road trip. He was a great help. He also was a good medic and knew how and what to do with casualties. I asked for him several times when I went out on the road.

My last road trip with D Company Nineteenth Combat Engineer Battalion was a trip I will never forget. We almost lost half the company on this last trip. We were going down the road as we always do. The new group of the Midnight Riders had went down the road about five to seven hours before, and we did not hear from them, so we thought everything was okay. Another convoy of APCs also went down the road from the Fifth Calve, and they never called for help. So our unit set out and went down the road, and we got about twenty miles, and we met up with the Fifth Calve unit.

They were ambushed by the enemy. There twelve APCs had casualties, and we only had four medics with us, so we started spreading out among the twelve APCs. We found out their medics had been wounded. We had eight casualties of our own of the twenty-three casualties we took care that day. We had to call in fire support on the area for we were still getting fired at. We got that situation cleaned up and started back on down the road mine sweeping and went about forty-five miles and ran into another ambush of snipers and had to call in more air support for that location.

We sustained four more casualties of our own, which had to be medivac to battalion aid for further treatment. So far, we had lost twelve soldiers from our ranks of what we brought with us on this trip. We were discouraged, but we went on doing our job because we knew that more troops were coming to replace what was lost in battle. As we went a little further down the road, we met up with the Midnight Riders alongside the road. Two of the tanks had hit a mine planted in the road, and the others were pulling security while they were trying to fix the tracks that were blown off their rollers. They had a few wounded soldiers, and we dressed their wounds, and they continued to work on their tank. We stayed with them till they were ready to leave again. It was a long eighty-one miles, and now we had to return home.

On the way back home, we got hit by another attack by the enemy. This time, it was a large-scale attack with mortar shells and a lot of enemy gunfire. The enemy were even coming out onto the road. The Quad 50s we had with us were firings right alongside the road. It was loud and noisy to my ears. Air support was dropping all kinds of shells at the enemy, and they were running away as fast as they could go. We still had several casualties to take care of on both sides. We had thirty of our own and fifty or more of the enemy soldiers—dead or wounded. We medivac twenty of our soldiers and twelve of the enemy soldiers to battalion aid for further treatment. The rest was sent to grave registration.

When we got back to the post that night, I found out that over half of the unit had been wiped out. The unit that stayed behind was also hit with an enemy motor attack and sustained heavy casualties. Thank goodness for air support or the whole unit would have been wiped out. The medics that were left and the personnel left had a long day preparing bodies for grave registration. We also had to get our compound back in order for it was in shambles from all the action that had happened.

I also found out that I had been reassigned to another unit and that I would be leaving in the morning. It did not give me much time to pack and say goodbye to all who was left in the company. I would be going to C Company First of the Twenty-third AMERICAL Infantry Division. It was a company made up to pull secret missions and to pull security in the mountains when the engineers are out on the roads working and doing other things like building bridges.

My last night in the company was quiet but exciting as it would go. There was a roll call called for and held in the mess hall. I did not expect at all. The company commander had a meeting with the company to announce that the departure of one of their personnel leaving for another duty assignment of greater importance signed by the division commander.

He said, "This special assignment will cause this person to be promoted and placed in a position of authority but also in a position of danger. This soldier has proven to be worthy to be able to meet the challenges set before him. Sergeant Robert Swan will be leaving us tomorrow as an SP6 or SSG Medical Supervisor."

I was shocked that I was picked out of the battalion to be the one to be transferred to the new division and promoted to do the job I soon would be doing. I knew not where I was going or what I would be doing. I would soon find out.

CHAPTER 7

Assignment Unexpectedly Changed in Middle of a Bad Time

Section I: Transferred to the C Company Twenty-Third Americal Infantry Division

Like I said, after my last mine sweep trip with the engineers, I got transferred to the C Company of the Twenty-Third Americal Infantry Division. They were stationed in the mountains twenty miles from Pleiku in land and to the west of the core area of Viet Nam. It was a place called LZ Thunder. It was set up pretty much the same way LZ Debbie was, except that it had a bigger and better field aid station built there and it was at a much higher location in a mountainous area.

It was completely surrounded by a fence and had guard towers every fifty feet around the whole compound. It was the first chain of evacuation for casualties. All patients would come to the field aid station before being medivac to the hospital. It was equipped to take care of minor surgical procedures if needed and other things a medic could not do out in the field. I had been promoted to SP 5 and now to be SP 6 senior in command of the medical platoon. We had thirty medics in the company, and we would go out on patrol with different squads of infantrymen and go to different locations in the mountains and along the road to pull security for the combat engineers that were working on the roads and building bridges.

I cannot tell you all the areas we were at for it would be a breach of security, but I can say we were sent into some pretty hot places. We were once on a mountain ridge and about half mile from the road. We were walking along a path with about twelve soldiers including myself. A sergeant I will call Best was about sixty feet ahead of me and turn around and called for me, and I started walking toward him. And I saw him walking toward me, so I stopped. When he got about twenty feet from me, he stepped on an anti-personnel mine. And it blew him apart, and pieces blew into me, sticking into my side knocking me over.

Parts of him were everywhere. I told the squad to take cover, and I had to control a new soldier who was on his first mission. He went into a fit because he was so scared as ever. I knelt down and told the soldier that God will take care of Sergeant Best and we can only be thankful that we had the chance to know such a hero as he was to his country. We can also be grateful that God spared the rest of us from danger. I had the radioman to call grave registration to meet us on the road with a litter and a body bag so we could carry Sergeant Best's remains out of the mountains. May he rest in peace.

There was another time when we were in the mountains pulling security, and I was sitting on a very large and high rock reading a Book of Mormon (I was a member of the Church of Jesus Christ of Latter-day Saints). I had not been to church since I came to Vietnam, but I was given this book by my primary teacher, Sister Townson. The name was changed to give privacy to the original person. She told me when I was young that if I read this book, I would build a testimony in it and I would be protected from harm because God would help me out if I believed in him and asked him to help me.

While I was reading the book, a soldier was sitting at the bottom of the rock poking his knife into the ground and under the rock. I stopped reading and started watching him for a while. He soon pulled up some wires from under the rock and that did not look right. He said for me to get down from the rock. The sergeant-in-charge called the engineer unit in the area to come and check the situation out. They showed up and put three-fourths pound of C-4 explosive under the rock with a lead wire of about four hundred yards long. We all got back the four hundred yards, and they lit the fuse.

When the C-4 went off, the rock I was lying on blew into a million pieces, and it left a hole twenty feet deep and forty feet in diameter. The engineers said it had to be a bomb, at least a fifty pounder under that rock. They also found wires going down the mountain on the other side. The enemy could have blown it at any time, but we found it in time. It was another miracle from God saving our lives. I believe it was because I was reading the Book of Mormon at the time that the wires were found. I thank God anyway for saving my life again.

As our squad was heading back to post from being out in the jungle and mountains for several weeks, we stopped to rest for a little bit. We were not there long before we started getting sniper fire. We took cover and located the source of where the fire was coming from. The enemy shot a rocket-propelled grenade toward us, and lo and behold, it landed right between my feet and did not go off, praise to God, or I would not be here to write this down. We were able to subdue the snipers, and we left the area fast before any more came along.

We were walking down the road, and we were crossing a bridge that had been damaged once and the engineers had fixed when a group of Vietnamese girls came walking across the bridge from the other direction. The soldiers in the squad started snickering at them and making jokes and calling them over to talk to them. They were getting upset, and they came over to our side where we were and started pushing me and pushed me over the bridge. I had not said anything to them, but I was the one they attacked. The bridge was seventy-five feet off the ground to the water. I was not a good swimmer, and when I went under the water, I went into a bunch of barbed wire from the old bridge that was damaged.

I was struggling to get out, and struggling was not helping. Then suddenly, a hand reached down into the water and took my hand and pulled me out of that tangled up barbed wire mess. When I got to the top and to the shore, there was no soldier around. I was alone to get out of the water with the squad on top of the bridge looking at me with an amazing glow in their eyes as if they could not believe what they just witnessed. I knew who saved me from that watery grave if the squad did not. I knew that I was being watched over as I had been promised years before if I would just believe.

Each day made me believe that much more in my Savior God to thee. I only prayed I can show him how much I cared and loved him by helping these soldiers get home the best way they can to their loved ones. I, Robert, love them all. As they all watched me climb back up the bank to the road, they all had a white face and a wondering glow. I, Robert, knew they wanted to ask how in the world I got out of that entangled mess, but I am sure they knew as I, Robert, did who it was that got me out for it was written on their faces. God never seizes to do miracles in the strangest places, even in the middle of a river of barbed wire.

CHAPTER 8

Secret Trips Our Unit Went on in the Jungle

Section I: Secret Missions in Jungle Where Agent Orange Was Used Against Us

We went on a secret mission, which I cannot reveal the whereabouts of it because I do not know myself. I only know that it was in the jungle somewhere. We traveled several days to get to where we needed to be. We met up with other units in the area and combined forces to increase our offensive attack on a certain position of the enemy's stronghold where they were keeping prisoners of war.

Our mission was to try and rescue the prisoners. Before we got there, we were attacked with a small group of enemy soldiers using Agent Orange. They used it in a mortar attack at us. We had several direct casualties from the chemicals and fragments that hit some soldiers directly, and they were medivac to the company aid station. The only thing about Agent Orange is that it can injure a person's inside for years to come. It eats away at the muscle, bone, joints, brain, vessels, and just about everything until the patient's limb is lost or they die from the disease. So anyone of us that was exposed to it could have problems later on in life. Time will only tell what will happen to each of us soldiers on this mission. It could be a year before we have any reaction.

We continued our mission and freed forty soldiers who had been held prisoners of war for over a year or more. I cannot mention any names, but there were some important people in the group. The mission took about two to three weeks to perform. And the walk back was not a picnic for we got hit with another ambush by the enemy, and we sustained several casualties, which we medivac to company aid. We had to carry casualties sometimes several miles in order to find a place that we might have enough clearance for a chopper to come in to pick up or patients to take to the battalion aid station in turn to prepare them to be medivac to the field and clearing hospitals, according to their injuries.

This mission cost us the lives of ten very good and heroic soldiers to grave registration and five to be sent to the hospital to be sent home. We saved the lives of forty soldiers from being prisoners of war, so by statistics, we did okay. But it hurt to lose anyone. I just pray that the good Lord will bless each of those brave soldiers who gave their lives for their country they loved and be with their families also.

When we got back to post, I was so tired I thought I could sleep for a week, but that was out of the question. I was informed that in six hours, we were heading back out to go on another mission of unknown destination. Oh well, I got a couple hours of sleep before I had to go back out. Why was I always going out on missions with thirty medics in our company, and I was in charge of all of them. They were going out on other missions that I have not been telling you about. I cannot tell you all about all the action that our company was involved in for it was just too extensive and would fill volumes. Some were left to run the aid station.

I went out on several missions that the commander wanted me to go on so I would be able to direct the medical treatment and affairs of the selected people we picked or helped to escape the prisoner of war camps they were in. Now back to the mission at hand.

This time, we went in a different direction but still toward the jungle. We did not know where we were going. We only had the coordinates to where to go. We went deep into the jungle for what seemed several days, and then we stopped to camp each night for a week or two. It was dark out, but we were told no lights. We had to rely on the moon and stars for light. Thank God for that. Then in the morning, we would start out again at dawn, walking more till we got to where we were going. We had not encountered any enemy at this point of our trip, and that seemed strange.

We were about a mile from a large bridge that looked like it was used to transport enemy troops from one area to another. We could see a compound or post in the distant on a mountainside that looked like an enemy compound. We did not have enough manpower to take on a compound that size. We would have to call in for air support and artillery support. If the plan were to blow the bridge, we would also need some combat engineer support. It would take some time to get it all set up to blow the bridge, so we had to hide out in the jungle while we waited for the engineers.

While we were waiting for an enemy patrol came down the road and across the bridge, they got out of their truck about one-fourth of a mile from our location and were looking around but did not see us at the time. So they started walking the opposite direction from us. We were safe for a while. The engineers got there, and we were able to start heading toward the bridge. It was a good size bridge made up of wood rails and metal from what looked like tank sides and tracks and parts of APCs and all kinds of things that seemed to be carried off from the location where the engineers would perform their mine sweep on the road south of LZ Debbie.

The bridge was about 175 feet long and about 50 feet off the ground. The road was made of hard-packed rock and dirt. It traveled in a north and south direction. The enemy compound was on the side of a mountain about a half mile away with a fence around it. We could see two or three guard towers around the front side of the compound. They had guards with machine guns in them from what we could tell with our field glasses. We thought we would call in an air strike on the compound at the same time we were putting explosives to the bridge. It would knock out two places at once. We were planting the explosives when we observed a convoy coming down the road toward us. We had to retreat into the jungle a little bit and wait for the air strike to hit the compound.

When it did, we pushed the plunger down on the charges of C-4 at the bridge, and the bridge blew into a million parts, also part of the convoy that was on the bridge now. From the looks of things, the place was in shambles, and we did not stick around to assess all the damage. We made it back to our post in about eight or nine days, and we did not have one casualty. Thanks to God that was our first mission without any casualties. He was looking out for us.

After this last battle with the enemy, I was tired, so I sat down and wrote this poem or message out for all and those back home who have wondered what it was like to face the enemy and may never return home. It is called A DATE TO KNOW.

I THINK EVERY MAN IN VIETNAM
WONDERS WHEN HIS TIME WILL COME
"WHAT WILL IT BE? A B40, RPG, AK47?
WHAT'S GOING TO SEND ME TO HELL OR HEAVEN?
WILL IT BE QUICK OR PAINFUL AND SLOW?
WHAT'LL IT BE LIKE WHEN I GO?"
NOT A MAN OVER HERE WANTS TO DIE
QUESTIONS TORTURE HIS MIND TO WHY
MANY MEN THINK THEY DON'T CARE
"IT'S GONNA HAPPEN SO WHY FEAR?
BE IT A BULLET HERE OR A CAR IN THE STATES
YOU'VE STILL GOT A DATE AT THE PEARLY GATES"
SO KEEP YOUR LUCKY CHARM AND SAY A PRAYER
'CUZ WHEN IT'S TIME THE ANGELS IN HEAVEN WILL
COME FOR YOU TO TAKE YOU HOME TO BE WITH THE
FATHER

Section 2: R&R to Da Nang Air Force Base to Attend LDS Church Conference

When we got back to our post, I was one tired person. I felt like I was in dire need of a rest, but I did not know how to get any around here. I heard that soldiers were taking in country R&R to get a way for just a few days, so I thought I might try and put in for one. I did not know where to go because most of the soldiers around here just wanted to get drunk and chase women, and that was not me.

I heard about a church conference at Da Nang Air Force Base for the LDS Church. I decided that is where I wanted to go after I prayed about it. I had a friend at LZ Debbie who was a member of the church and wondered if he would be there at the conference. I was approved to go. So in the first weekend in October of 1968, I went by helicopter to Da Nang Air Force Base.

When I got there, I found out that the base was divided into two sections: a north and a south base. I believe it might have been east and west. I am not sure. It has been over fifty years since I have been there. I do know that it was early Saturday morning and there was no transportation to the other side. The only means of transportation was by heli-copter, and they were grounded on the weekend except for emergencies. There was a guard gate beside the edge of main base and a section of road leading to the other base. I did not want to get stopped because the guard would not let me through without some form of transportation. So I hid my gun and rifle in the tall grass along the fence line about three hundred yards from the guard gate.

I climbed the fence and went through some woods and some large rocks till I got to the road. I then started sing-ing church songs for some reason. I passed through what I thought was a large village. There were several mama-sans and papa-sans in black pajamas and several children running around. The children came up to me, and I gave them some candy bars that I had with me. I kept going, but the par-ents just looked at me like I was the strangest thing they've ever seen, walking through their village. I noticed there were weapons standing or leaning up a long side of their huts.

I just kept singing and walking down the road till I got to the other side of the base where there was another guard gate. I could not avoid it. It came on me to fast, and they saw me coming down the road. When I got to the gate, they asked me where I came from. I told them I came from the other side. They then ask where I was going. I told them I was going to an LDS conference. They then ask if I knew anyone there. I said no. Then they put me in a strait jacket and told me to sit down.

They called the area where the conference was going to be held and asked if someone would come to the gate to talk to them and me. Two gentlemen showed up at the gate and talked with the military police or gate guards at the gate. They told the gentlemen the story I told them, and they told them the situation with the road and the village. They could not believe I made it down that road and through the village with the road full of mines and the village full of North Vietnam regular army soldiers and sympathizers and their families. Then they told them that they heard me singing church songs from a long way off like all I had on my mind was God and this conference. They told the gentlemen, they thought I was nuts.

The gentlemen said, "Let us talk to him, and we will let you know." They came over to talk to me and introduced themselves to me and asked who I was. I told them who I was and where I came from—the unit anyway. Later I told them I was from Iowa. They asked why I wanted to come to the conference. I gave them my testimony of what I believed to be true about the church and about God and Jesus Christ. I told them what I had been through since I had been in Vietnam. I told them I know that God and Jesus Christ had saved my life on many occasions because I had been reading the scriptures and praying to him asking for his help in making the right decisions so I could help the wounded soldiers to get back to the hospital where they could get the help they needed, to be sent home to their families. I told them that God and Jesus were answering my prayers.

I was trying my hardest to be what he wanted me to be. I told them about my primary teacher and her promise to me. I was trying to live my life to fulfill that promise she made to me. They went and told the guards that they would take care of me and they would take me to the conference. They also said I was not a nut case but full of faith for God and Jesus Christ and he or I was willing to sacrifice his or my life to attend this conference.

When I got to the conference, I enjoyed it so much that I started crying because it touched me inside so much. One of the gentlemen came up to me and laid his hand on my shoulder and said he would like to interview me to become an elder in the Holy Melchizedek Priesthood. This person's name was Ezera Taft Benson. He was the Southern Far East Mission president at the time. He later became president of the Church of Jesus Christ of Latter-day Saints. I was ordained an elder in the same church by the other gentlemen who came to the gate. His name was W. Brent Hardy who later became one of the twelve apostles for the Lord Jesus Christ here on earth.

My friend from LZ Debbie was there to welcome me into the Elders Quorum of the church. He was already an elder. I was at the conference through Sunday afternoon and had the most spiritual experience I have ever had in my life. I will never forget that weekend as long as I shall live.

When I got back to the other side of the base, I retrieved my weapons and equipment and was able to get a helicopter back to my unit on Monday morning. I will never forget this experience while I am still alive. It was the best thing or experience I had while serving in Vietnam. I learned a lot in such a short period of time. I am ready for the next challenge that I will go through while I am over here because I know that the Lord is on my side. I will trust in his judgement to lead me or help me to make the best choice I can giving the situation we are in.

CHAPTER 9
Last Firefight for Me as a Whole Man

We still had to go out on several secret missions in the jungle, but they did not seem nearly as hard as before. We were there and back before our beds got cold. We had very few problems with injuries. We had two sniper fires where two people got shot with minor wounds. One was me, and it was just a small flush wound under my left breast where a bullet creased my skin. The sniper was taken into custody and put in and army jail in South Vietnam some where I do not know where. We turned him over to the military police. It had turned to be a cold and snowy winter season, and the holidays were coming upon us. We did not go out on any missions. We stayed home regrouping and taking care of and fixing up our equipment for when we would go out the next time.

It looked like we were going to have a real cold and snowy white Christmas. We sang songs in the mess tent and drank hot chocolate with whipped cream. The next day it was back to the same duty of going out on a mission and not knowing where we were going. This time, it took twenty-seven days to get there with camping in the jungle at night. The place was creepy looking and really closed off from others to find. It was also cold outside with snow on the ground, making our mission that much more difficult to handle and accomplish. It reminded me of an area that prisoners might be in somewhere and we have come to find them and rescue them. Sure, enough that was our mission.

We were told that a prison camp was about one to two miles further into the jungle across a large bridge with guard enclosures every 50 feet of the 150-foot bridge. Our job was to wait for the air strike on the bridge. Once the bridge enclosures were wiped out, we would cross the bridge and mount an offense on the prison camp and retrieve the seventy-five to a hundred Americans prisoners and help them back across the bridge. We then would help take them back to a safe area by any means possible. We had the air force and their transport planes equipped standing by about ten miles away waiting for us to arrive at their landing site to load the Americans who were being held prisoners of war so the American prisoner could aboard the plane to go home.

We only sustained twelve wounded soldiers during this stage of the process. We then medivac the wounded soldiers to the division field clearing station hospital, and three were actual sent back to the clearing station hospital in North English where they would be heading home to the States. The others were sent back to our unit in about ten days from the division field clearing station hospital. They only needed minor surgery and a little recovery period. We got back to our post without problems.

It was after the New Year now, and snow was on the ground. The cold was bitter, and we had to wear extra clothing to stay warm. But that did not always help. We still had to move around a lot just to keep our circulations going. We did not go out on any more secret missions because of the bitter cold. We did go out and pull security for the engineer companies that was still engaged in doing mine sweeps on the highways through the mountains. They had to keep them open for the convoys that were taking equipment through the mountain passes. It was cold but it had to be done, and it was not without problem with mines explosions because of the cold weather or someone's slipping on or off the road and going over the edge of the mountain and having problems getting back on the road or a sniper fire attack causing a panic and people getting hurt from it.

Section 2: Blown Out of Jeep Over and Down a Mountain a Long Way About Four Hundred to Six Hundred Feet

It was about five to six month, I think, after I returned from R&R that we had a second big or high mission to go on. We were taking a convoy of vehicles down the road to a certain point. Then we were going to dismount and walk to a location unknown to us at the time. We were traveling through a canyon with a high mountain range. I was riding in a jeep with a Quad 50-caliber machine gun mounted on it. I had a hundred-pound rucksack and an eighty-pound aid bag on my back. I also had two bandannas around my shoulder to my waist with six to eight dressings attached to each of them.

I had my field jacket tied around my waist in case it got cold at night, and my rain gear and poncho were in my rucksack. I also had a month supply of small food items plus other food item extra in case someone was short of food. I wore my pistol belt with three canteens of water and several dressings and first aid ointment iodine, etc. My aid bag was full of first aid equipment and tools for whatever I needed to do minor surgery. I had IV solution and whatever it took to keep a patient's body fluids going. We did not know how long we would be gone. All the soldiers carried a lot of gear.

While we were in the canyon, the convoy was attacked by a band of enemy gorillas with lots of enemy soldiers with heavy gunfire and mortar rounds. The jeep I was riding in jerked around so it could fire the quad 50s at the enemy. As it was turning around, it hit a mine planted in the road, and I went flying out of the jeep and over the side of the mountain and down the side. It was a long way down. I want to say about four hundred to six hundred feet through trees and rocks and brushes and everything else that is in the mountains.

When I hit the bottom, I could still hear heavy gunfire from several kinds of weapons like M16s, AK47s, machine guns, mortar rounds. I even heard a grenade or two go off. I heard an air strike over head but could not see it from where I was lying. I hoped that the air strike did some good. It sounded bad, but it was a faint sound to me from where I was. There were several explosions. I was having problems hearing things, and I could not move. I felt numb from my waist down. I also felt very weak and lightheaded like I was going to pass out.

My head was ringing, and my mouth was bleeding. I had a hole in the side of my face and my lower jaw. My legs were also bleeding, and my right shoulder was hurting like crazy. My whole body was hurting like it had been torn apart. I landed on my aid bag and rucksack, and it felt like they had taken most of the impact, which saved my life. They kind of acted like a cushion and saved me from a broken back. I am sure my legs were messed up because I could hardly move them at first, but they did get a little movement in them so I could crawl later.

Section 3: Ambush Continued for More Than Several Hours

As I laid at the bottom of the mountain, I could still hear some explosions and some of the guns fire from the fire-fight at the top of the mountain that was still going on. It did not sound good for anyone. It went on for several hours before there was complete silence from the firing of weapons. I did not hear no sounds at all from vehicles on the road. I wondered if there was anyone still up there. I did not want to yell in case the enemy might still be in the area. I waited for someone to come down and try and find me, but after several hours, I gave up hope of anyone coming to find me. I just wondered if they all got wiped out or did they just forget about me because of all the fighting that was going on and the one that survived took off fast back toward the compound.

Section 4: No One Came to Get Me or See If I Was All Right, Was I Dead or Alive?

Absolutely no one came down the mountain to see if I was still alive or all right. I could not believe they would just leave me all alone without at least checking on me. There had to be a serious problem for them to do that. I would venture to guess that the company was pretty wiped out and who-ever made it out left fast. I had heard someone before asking, "Where is Doc Swan? We need him badly. We have a lot of soldiers that need taken care of."

And someone told them, "He had been blown over the mountain and is probably dead at the bottom of the mountain because of the long fall. He was probably blown to pieces by the mine explosion and thrown from the quad 50 jeep explosion. Grave registration will have to come and find his parts if they can."

So I knew they were not going to come and look for me at all. I was on my own to get out of this place. I would have to devise a plan of survival and try to evade the enemy at all cost. My goal was to get back to my unit the best way I could and the fastest so I did not freeze or starve or bleed to death.

Help me, Lord find the way to survive this ordeal and lead me to the path I need to go to find my way back to my company or where I my find help indeed.

Section 5: They Must Have Had Reasons Why Not to Check On Me

I must have passed out for a while for when I started moving around, it was quiet. The next thing I knew I woke up and it was dark out and very quiet. I did not hear any more gunfire from on top of the mountain or any vehicles moving around. There was no one moving, talking or yelling, for me or trying to find me. I did not know what happened to any of the rest of the convoy. I knew I had to get into some shelter to hide from the enemy before they found me.

I pulled all my strength I could manage together even though I had a very badly wounded left leg, but I started crawling very slowly in what I thought was the direction toward our post. I tried to crawl for what I thought was about an hour going in and out and around trees to stay hidden from sight, from being seen by the enemy. I must have crawled about a few miles or so till I found a good bunch of bushes that I could crawl in so I could go to sleep. I was so weak, and my legs hurt badly. My head hurt, and my mouth was bleeding. I had lost some teeth. I had a small bullet hole in the left side of my face and a little bigger hole in my right lower jaw. My gums were torn up some and bleeding where I had to put some gauze in my mouth to try and stop the bleeding.

I had some food with me, but I did not eat because I was in pain. I needed a doctor, but that would have to wait. I tried to go to sleep for a while, but with the pain, it was really hard to go to sleep for a long time. So it was cat naps all night long. The next morning when I awoke, I heard a noise, and I listened real quietly to what it was. It was a group of enemy soldiers passing by going down a path toward where we had the firefight. I am so glad they did not see me in the bushes or I would have been caught right then. Thank you, Jesus, for saving me again.

After the enemy had got out of sight for a while, I decided to move out to a new location and started out again in the direction I was going. I changed the dressings I had put on the night before and put them in my aid bag because I did not want anyone to know I had been there, and I was going to wash the dressing material out with water and dry it so I could reuse the dressing material. I tried to eat something soft from my aid bag. I had some soft cookies, so I ate three of them with some juice that I had brought from a V-8 can. It was all I could manage to get down. My, stomach was still upset from the fall.

I crawled about four to five hours, taking breaks every hour for about fifteen to twenty minutes. I then would crawl for three to four hours more doing the same kind of breaks. I did this type crawling all day long till I got so tired I had to find a place where I could rest for a while or the night. I did not think I could go any further that day, plus I needed to clean my dressings and wash my bandages and eat something.

There were some small salamanders in a moist bed of leaves and mud, so I managed to capture six to seven of them and put them in a V8 can I had drunk the juice out of. They would not be in the can that long because I would be able to use them for food the next two days. I could not cook them, but I could put them in salt water and cut their heads off and just put them in my mouth and swallow them down then eat some crackers behind it as a chaser so the salamander would go down then I would take a drink of water to wash it all down.

I felt like I was about gone and on my last breath. I hurt so much. I was moving on sheer will power. I had to find a hiding spot. Then I would start in again tomorrow. When I took my breaks each day while I was crawling, I did eat some of the food I had and drink what water I had. I did this for several days and months. It was hard to keep track of time because I was scared what was around the next corner for me. I was only praying that God was my copilot and he would lead me in the right way to safety.

I knew I was lost, and by now, I was sure considered missing or killed in action. On one occasion, I was desperate for some food I crawled into a small village store and stole some crackers and small food items. I did leave a five-dollar bill on the floor and left. A mama-san saw me and did not say anything but waved her hand to me as I left. That night while I was I was crawling back in my bed, I was visited by a person tugging at my boots as if he were trying to take them off me. I tried pull my feet in under the bushes, but they hurt just too much. I opened up my make-shift tent or enclosure to see who was trying to get my boots.

I saw that it was a single Vietnam soldier older man who looked like he had been all by himself for quite a spell. His uniform was all worn out, and his shoes or boots were all torn up. No wonder why he wanted my boots. I pointed to him to come in and sit down so we could talk. I gave him something to eat because it looked like he had not eaten in days. He ate and drank some juice. I took my shoes off and gave them to him, and I took his and showed him that I had bad legs and was crawling so I did not really need shoes to crawl.

I asked him if he could speak any English, and he told me just a little bit. I asked if he knew where the nearest army unit was so I could get treated or hospital. I needed it bad. I have been crawling and lost for a long time now. I knew he did not have a weapon, so he could not harm me. So I was not scared of him, and he seemed not to be scared of me. When he was ready to leave, he said, "Thank you and good bye and good luck. Hope to see you soon." I did not see him again then he was gone.

I said to him, "My prayers are with you."

On another night while I was lying still in my make-shift bed made of bush and leaves and blanket and field jacket, I had another visit from a predator called a bamboo viper (a poisonous snake). Luckily, I had seen it when it come into my enclosure so I could hit it with my Machete knife and cut its head off before it tried to bite me. I found the knife as I was crawling my way through the jungle or mountainous terrain as I call it. Thank God for saving my life again. For without that knife, I would have been bitten by the most poisonous snake in Vietnam. It is also known as the Three Stepper for those who usually get bit die with in taking three steps.

Section 6: Crawled Many Miles on My Hands and Knees Trying to Stay Ahead of the Enemy

CHAPTER 10

Missing in Action

Section I: Missing in Action and Found
by a South Vietnam Army Unit and Put in
Their Hospital after Being Lost for Over
Twenty-Four Months in the Jungle

You will see that some of this area that it looks like it has already had been written, and it may have been. But due to the mental status of myself during the period of time, it was important to repeat the facts that will show just how hard it was to survive out in the jungle on your own for over twenty-four months, crawling all over the place and not finding anything that looked like it was around our post.

It had been several months, and I was almost out of food and water. I had started using my IV solution saline to drink as water from my aid bag, and I resorted to eating berries and scrubs when I could find them. I even ate a few worms at times and some small lizards (salamanders). I did not want to but was desperate, so I crawled into some villages to some stores and tried taking a few food items from them to survive. I think they saw me and did not say anything because they knew I was hurt. It was cold, so it was hard to crawl around and not very far at a time. I had to try and sleep during the day and do my cleaning of my wounds and tightening up my splints on my legs so I could continue to crawl through this jungle canopy.

I did my crawling mainly in the afternoon after the sun was not so hot and at night for protection from the enemy. I had clothing and blanket in my rucksack. I am so thankful the Lord was with me and gave me a hint to be prepared for this mission. I listened to him, and I am still alive and warm right now because of him. I was able to avoid the enemy patrols that went through the area at times by covering up in my blanket under the bushes. I continued to eat what I could off the ground that was eatable least it kept me alive. I ran out of IV solution, so I used rainwater and muddy water and put some water purification tablets in it to kill germs so it would be drinkable. I had some tablets in my aid bag. Like I said, the Lord prepared me for this mission for he knew it was going to be rough on me.

I prayed to him often to thank him for his help each day and each step or crawl of the way. I must have been out in the woods or mountains jungle for at least twenty-three to twenty-four months or so—give or take a month. I was marking the days with a pen I had on my ruck sack. I am not sure of the accuracy of the count, but I counted 454 days that when I broke my pen. I could not mark my bag anymore since I broke it on that 454th day. I just started crawling day by day after that. I tried to on a day-by-day to remember or estimate the days I crawled.

It was I think on Day 521. I was hiding under the bushes with my blanket over me when I heard a noise, and I tried to peek out to see what it was. I saw a small group of soldiers standing by the bush I was under. They were talking and pointing down towards me. I was afraid they were going to shoot me. They pulled me out from under the bush and saw that I was wounded. I also saw the North Vietnam soldier I had given my boots to standing with the South Vietnam soldiers who were pulling me out from under the bushes.

The North Vietnam soldier had brought the other soldier to me to save my life and to take me to their hospital area. The North Vietnam soldier waved his hand at me. He had actually saved my life by getting the other soldiers to come and get me. He also turned himself in at the same time to them. It is kind of ironic that that I preform a good deed for an enemy soldier that he might live and he in turn found the help that would save my life. I hope and pray that that soldier tells his family someday that he was saved by an American soldier as I can say I was saved by a North Vietnam Soldier. It does not always work out that way.

Section 2: South Viet Nam Hospital Put Me Back Together the Best They Could with What They Had to Work With

A lump came in my throat because I thought I had been caught by the enemy. A patrol of South Vietnam Soldiers was standing right in front of the bush I was at, and they saw me. They took me out of my hiding place and seen that I was injured. They tried to talk to me, but I could not understand them. They put some clean dry warm dressings on some of my wounds, and they made a litter using my blanket. They placed me on the litter gently as not to further injure my legs. They then took my field jacket and covered me up with it and started carrying me through the mountains and jungles.

The North Vietnam soldier walked right along the side of the litter just looking at me as if to say, *We are going home.* He held my hand for assurance that he would stay with me all the way. In about fourteen to fifteen days, they arrived at their hospital area. I am sure it was close to the Cambodia border where they took me to their doctors who took me right in and started taking care of my wounds. I found out I had a broken right shoulder bone with an AC separation of the right arm, and I had been crawling using my arms. No wonder it hurt.

My face was skinned up a lot and had a small bullet hole in the left side of the face. The bullet went in and tore up my upper teeth and gums, then it turned downward toward and tore out some lower teeth and gums and came out the through the lower right jaw making a little larger hole. They did a graph on my face and jaw, and you can hardly tell where the exit point was now. They started but could not finish rebuilding my mouth and gums. So I could only start sipping liquids. I could not eat anything after they started working on my mouth. They removed all kinds of metal particles from my legs and back as well as rock and splinters.

They also set my broken legs with casts and put bamboo pins in my legs. I also had my fifth and sixth vertebrae damaged to the point where they had to put me in a neck brace hoping it would heal back together. They did try and wire it back together with a pin and the brace the best they could. I could not speak their language, and they could not speak English. They had no one who could speak both languages, so they had to wait till they could get one in to send me to an army hospital.

They did their best to be quite friendly helpful and kind. They took real good care of me. I was there about seven to eight months, I guess, before they got someone in that could speak English. He came and talked to me and asked me where I was stationed at. I told him, and they asked where the hospital was for our area. And I told them. They then called for a medivac to the military hospital, and in four days, I was on my way to the army Hospital in North English. It was in the middle of South Vietnam. That meant that I had been missing in action for over thirty-one months till the time I got to the army hospital in North English.

CHAPTER 11

Got an Interpreter, Assigned to Unit

Section 1: Helped Get Me Transferred to US Army Unit North English

Yes, I was sent to an army hospital in North English. It was about 250 miles or so south of our location or post. There was an air force Hospital closer, I think, but I guess if they thought since I was an army and I had to go to an army hospital. That is why I ended up in North English.

I was still weak from being in the Vietnam hospital. I had lost a lot of weight and had stomach trouble. I felt sick a lot and feverish often, and I do not know why unless it was because I was exposed to Agent Orange several times in my travels. I was so tired and exhausted that I just wanted to sleep for a long periods of time but knew I had to keep going and not let the Grim Reaper creep in and take me. I prayed often to relax and to find guidance from the Good Lord in how to survive the situation I was in. He helped me always have a good spirit and a willingness to survive.

It was hard but I kept losing weight, and I was not eating too much food. It just did not taste very good, and when they started working on my mouth, I did not get to eat any more, just drink liquids. I needed some down-to-earth, good old-fashioned, home-style Mom's cooking to straighten me out. This army slop they try to serve as food did nothing but cause pain and suffering and diarrhea most of the time. Yes, I was not a good patient because I was not feeling good at all.

Section 2: Doctors Informed Me I Was Labeled Killed in Action and I Would Have to Prove Who I Was in Order to Get Out of Vietnam!

When I got there, the doctor informed me that I had no identification and the records on me showed me being killed in action in the spring of 1969. This is now almost thirty-one months later. Where have I been? I told him the complete story of my last thirty-one months of life. He was so shocked, but he could tell by how malnourished I was. I was so unrecognizable because of my weight loss and my long hair and ugly looking wounds that I looked like death warmed over many times.

He asked how I was able to survive all those months. I told him that it was through the Lord's help and his wisdom in teaching me how to survive on the elements at hand and how to use them to the best of my ability. I thank Jesus every day for his love and guidance to help me through the roughest storms. He has saved my life many times, and I owe him my life big time.

The doctor and nurses did everything they could to get my body back in order, but there were things that just could not be cured like the Agent Orange that had destroyed genes in my head and destroyed my temperature control center of the brain and the degeneration of the bones of my brain and spinal cord. My equilibrium was totally messed up, and I could hardly walk straight, so I was put in crutches. I was put in the crutches to start with but was told I would end up in a wheelchair in a few years.

My backbone was breaking up also, so I was put on large amounts of calcium to build up my bones. They took more metal fragments from my legs that was coming to the surface. They said it would come festering up for years with the looks of my legs right now. They said they hoped that gangrene would not set in my legs. They treated me for an infection just the same for a precaution. I was there for several months also trying and hoping to prove who I was.

I tried writing letters to my battalion headquarters to see if there was anyone there that knew me, but no letters returned. I prayed that someone would respond to one of my letters. I must have written every day to someone I thought might be there. I did start feeling a little better after a few weeks of a better liquid diet with some food in it and healthy medical treatment. I know that the Vietnam hospital saved my life, and I am indeed grateful and thankful for their help. I will always treat them with the upmost respect.

The North Vietnam soldier that brought the hospital soldiers to my rescue, I will honor him as a hero and a true friend and hope he will be given impunity or freedom to be able to live in South Vietnam as a free man for the rest of his life with his family. He deserves the highest medal their government can bestow on a person for his bravery and heroic deeds in saving a life of a foreign soldier who would have died if it had not been for his heroic deeds in saving the soldiers life.

Section 3: A Master Sergeant Came to Hospital from the Battalion Where I Was from to Inform Me My Parents Were Notified of My Death over Two Years Ago

About four or five months after I was there, a soldier showed up from the battalion headquarters from where I was from. He had re-extended three times to stay in Vietnam. He was ready to go home. He had to have an evaluation from the division medical officer in charge to leave Vietnam since he had been there for quite a spell. He just happened to come through the ward I was in and saw me and was in shock. He came to me and said. "Is that you, Swan? I thought you were dead. Well, I even signed your death certificate and sent it home to your parents with your remains."

I said, "Wait a minute," and called for the doctor and let the master sergeant E-8 tell him the story. He told me to prove who I was and about the explosion over the side of the mountain that caused me to become missing in action or killed in action in action for so long. Thanks to God it was the later—just missing in action.

But all my records were messed up because I was considered as killed. Still that could be fixed with a lot of hard work and time in the service as well as in civilian life and in my financial matters. I remained in the hospital for another four or five months till the doctors were sure I was ready to return home to the States. I was still having a lot of nightmares and shell shock issues and was told I had post-traumatic stress disorder. There would have times that I would be afraid of my own shadow and hide from my fears instead of confronting them. Then other times I would strike out like a raging bull and try to fight my way to victory if I did not have something to calm me down.

Well, I had the Lord to help me, and he has kept me in check for a long time. If it were not for him, I would have gone crazy a long time ago. I have had a lot of close calls of deep depressions and anger disorders. It is not cool. I wake up at night just shaking and in a cold sweat, jerking so badly I seem not to be able to stop at times. I have jerked myself right out of my bed on to the floor or wherever I am at. It could be the ground because I have seen myself being blown over that mountain repeatedly hitting the ground with my head. I saw only stars in the sky and someone calling me saying, "Swan, where are you? Get yourself up here and fix these patients or they are going to die. It will be your fault, if they die."

I tried to move, but I cannot move. When I did not respond to the voice, in just a few minutes later, there were dead bodies being thrown down at me. The voices started telling me again that this was my fault for not coming up to do my job and to quit being a wimpy little soldier man. It really gets to you when you feel like you are a failure to yourself and to mankind and to the world. You feel all is lost to you when you lose your identity and your existence in the middle of a jungle all alone and not able to talk to anyone but the good Lord.

I know by all rights that I should have perished at the bottom of the mountain. By pure luck and faith, I was able to pull myself through some ridiculously hard and trying and unmanageable days of hell bending torture on my body. But with it the will of God, I was capable pulling every little bit of strength I could muster to keep myself going. I admit that if I had not been found when I was, it was really at my near end of my life. I was giving up slowly.

Section 4: Sent Home After Fifty-One Months of Being Missing in Action but Labeled as Killed in Action

It was over four years from when I went to Vietnam that now I finally was going back to the United States where I started from. I got to go home for a while. I had orders to go to Fort Dix, New Jersey. I did not know what it would be like working in a hospital or ambulance company. I was told I could be assigned to either place. It was along the Atlantic Coastline. It was close to New York.

When I boarded the plane in Vietnam, I was so happy to be alive that I thanked my God for all he did for me and saving my life so many times. I prayed for the other soldiers that were still there in Vietnam that they, too, might return home in safety if God saw fit that he had to take them home to him. I asked God to bless each one with the highest blessing he could give them. I really felt like I was deserting my fellow soldiers in arms who were fighting bravely for American freedom. They were serving their country well and were all heroes in my book.

The plane trip took forty-two hours to get back to Travis Air Force Base, State of Washington. From there, I got a plane to Des Moines, Iowa. Then I got a plane to Burlington, Iowa were my parents lived. I did not call my parents that I was coming come. I wanted to surprise them. It had been gone over four years since I saw them, so I know it would be a shock to them and to me. But I was not ready for what I was about to run into.

While I was on the plane, I met a news reporter from Des Moines who asked me where I was coming from and where I was going, so I told her my story about Vietnam and my parent thinking I had been killed in action. She liked the story and decided to travel to Burlington with me to see the reaction of my parents once they saw me after four years.

CHAPTER 12

Going Home

Section I: The Homecoming at the Airport

Like I said before, I never called my parents that I was coming home. I got to the Burlington Airport at about 6:00 a.m. on August 24, 1972, I believe. This was over four years after I left for Vietnam. The first thing I did, and people thought it kind of strange of me, was I bent down and kissed the ground of good old Iowa and said a prayer right there and then and thanked God for bringing me home as he promised he would. The News reporter just stood watching me and smiled at me. People looked at me like I was crazy and was having a fit. They asked me if I was all right. I told them that I was so honored to be home from Vietnam and that God made sure I made it home as he promised. They then spat at me and called me names, like baby killer and other harsh names.

I stood up and said to the people that I was proud to serve my country. "I spent the last forty-one months missing in action and labeled killed in action for my heroic actions. I have not seen my family in over four years, and you have the nerve to say I am a baby killer when I personally delivered nine babies of Vietnamese origin under enemy fire and was wounded doing so.

"I never asked to go to Vietnam, but by going, I know I am a much better man. I am going home to see my parents who think I am dead right now and explain what happened to me. You will hear about me in the future when I build up the nerve to write my book about my experience in the Republic of Vietnam. Then you will see how I really feel about my love for the USA and my friends and family. So then you will just have to hate me or get to know me, and my family because I am not going to change for anyone. I believe what I believe, and no one is going to take that from me."

Then the news reporter stated, "In the evening news, the eruption and welcoming of this hero will be publicized as a tribute to the unruliness of our society, This soldier gave his all for this town, and you give him a welcome back like this is? It so disgraceful. It is so immoral. It is outrageous to his character. You owe him your deepest apologies."

Section 2: Meeting My Parents after Four Years and After Them Thinking That I Am Dead

As we I walked home, I tried to remember all the things I wanted to say to my mom and stepdad when I got home, and I started crying because I had been gone so very long. I just did not know what I was going to tell them. I had written them and told them I was stationed in a hospital area and was safe from harm. But how was I going to explain my extended absence for so long a time? I know that people stay longer than usual at times but not over four years. No one is that good, so I could not use that excuse. I would have to tell them I had gotten sick and was in the hospital for a little while. But then they would ask why I did not write and tell them I was sick! Boy, I just could not come up with a good excuse that would explain my absence so long.

I decided to play it by ear and not say anything unless pressured into confessing. I finally got to Jefferson Street where they lived. It was still early morning about 8:00 a.m. I did not hear any noise at all around the place. The dogs were even being quiet. As we climbed the hill up to the backdoor of the back porch, we noticed the dogs were staring at us but not making a sound. It was like they were seeing a ghost and was in a trance of some kind.

We stepped in on the back porch and headed toward the backdoor. We noticed a makeshift room off to the right of me, and I looked in and saw my brother, Steve, sleeping soundly in a cot made just for him. I wanted to wake him but did not because he looked too peaceful in his slumber. We went to the backdoor and knocked on it gently, so we would not disturb Steve and his sleeping.

We heard someone coming toward the door, and when the door opened, it was my mother. She looked at me with a blank stare and then fell right between my feet. My stepfather came running out to see what was going on. When he saw me, he, too, went into a blank stare and fell right over mom on the floor. I bent down and started giving them mouth-to-mouth artificial respiration. I yelled for help, and the kids that were home came running, and I told them to call 911.

Section 3: Ambulance Called to Revive Mom and Stepdad

In just a few minutes, an ambulance was there giving my parents air by an oxygen machine, which brought them back to their senses. That was not the reception I was expecting. The paramedics got my parents up and sitting at the table, and we all sat down each around the end of the table. We all just stared at other for a little while. Then the paramedics asked, "What caused them to have such a reaction as they did?"

They turned to me and looked at me and said to me, "How are you here, and why? You are dead! The army came and told us you were killed in action a little over two years ago in combat and that your body would be shipped home to us shortly for burial with honors. I got scared and did not know just what to say!"

The news reporter introduced herself and said she met me on the plane coming to Iowa and was quite interested in my story also as to what really happened in Vietnam, and she relayed the incident at the Burling Airport—how I was totally mistreated in my homecoming welcome. She said she is going to put an article in the evening paper, so she had to leave. She called for a cab to come to pick her up. She said she just wanted to meet my parents to get my reaction of me being alive after so many years.

My mother got up and went toward the back of the house and then came back with a box about two feet by three feet and sat it down in front of me and said, "What is this?"

I opened the box and right on top was my death certificate, and the date was the date that I was blown over the mountain. They had labeled me killed in action that day instead of looking for me. The other stuff was metals and written letter about the heroic acts of bravery that were performed by me while serving with that unit and the money I had saved up to prepare to send home, which was $3,400 to give to mom for her needs with a last will and testament in the case something happened to me.

There was a letter to my girlfriend in Fort Polk, Louisiana, leaving her some money also and a painting I had painted of her to give her when we got married. She might not be able to see it now because she and her car were hit by an eighteen-wheeled truck. I was asked not to come because I would go crazy after what I already went through. I then had a hard sharp pain go through my left shoulder because my mother hit me with a broom stick hard.

She said, "How many times have I told you never to lie to me? And you lied to me, and you scared the whole family thinking you were dead. You were not working in no hospital but was in a jungle field unit and went on several top-secret missions that you got wounded in. You also saved people from getting hurt."

I told her I did not know that this was happening. I was missing in action for thirty-four months and spent about nine months to twelve months trying to prove who I was. I did not know they labeled me killed in action. I lived off the land, hiding from the enemy and trying to stay alive with all the wounds I had and broken bones I had. I had to crawl all over the jungle and mountains to hide from the enemy patrols that were in the area. It was not easy, and if it were not for God, I would have died out in the jungle and been eaten by wild animals and never been seen again. The Lord gave me power to survive the horrendous ordeal and helped me get home to my family as he promised he would do.

Section 4: Going Through Living-Room Window

As I was sitting at the kitchen table, I soon had to go to the bathroom to relieve myself of the liquid I had stored in my bladder. I stood up and started walking into the living room for the bathroom was in the back of the house toward Mom's bedroom. I hoped I could still hold it for I was hurting bad. When I got off the airplane, I had to go to the bathroom and did not go. I thought I could hold it till I got home.

I went to the bathroom and thought I was going to urinate myself for quite a while. Thank you, God, that I did not go in my clothing. I remember a case I had of a girl rupturing her bladder by holding her urine in too long. She said to me in a conversation that she just could not go to the bathroom back to the living room. While I was in, there was a couch that I had to pass that set in front of a bay window—a large bay window. I heard a loud noise like an explosion. I was so shell shocked that I jumped right through that bay window.

I rolled down the hill and dropped off the ledged and fell about ten feet right on top a hood of a car that had backfired that made the loud sound. I had hurt my back again, and it was sore again all over. The paramedics that was at the house for Mom and Dad came to my rescue and had to put me on a stretcher backboard and transport to the hospital for evaluation. I was in the hospital for about twelve hours then released.

Section 5: Placed in Hospital for Twelve Hours then Released

I already had a back injury from Vietnam. This fall on top of this car did not help. I was put in the Oskaloosa General Hospital for twelve hours because my back was hurting. They gave me some pain shots, took some blood test, and asked several questions. They told me that my blood test indicated that I might have an infectious disease coming on, but they did not know what it was right now. They said I could have picked up a bug in Vietnam. They said when I got to Fort Dix New Jersey to go in for a complete check-up. They said my back would be sore for a while, but it is not broken. But it is softening, so they started me on some calcium tablets twice a day to strengthen the bones.

When I went back home, I got some bad news that I did not want to hear. And it hit me very emotionally. The news ruined the rest of my leave I had coming because I just wanted to do nothing but be by myself. I was glad that I had my family to lean on for support or I just do not know what I would have done. I also had Heavenly Father to explain why things happen the way they do and why it makes us stronger. I am still saddened from the news and just not sure what to do about it.

Section 6: Told Not to Go to Fort Polk, Louisiana, to See Girlfriend

My mother got the call from Mrs. Smith (the name was changed to protect the innocent) from Louisiana while I was in the Oskaloosa General Hospital recovering from my fall from my mother's retaining wall at her house on Jefferson's street. She told my mother that her daughter had been in an accident with an eighteen-wheeler truck. The truck ran over her daughter's car with her daughter in it. She was not expected to survive maybe a week at most longer. It would be best with what I had been through that I not come and see her because I would go crazy. It would be best just to remember her as she was.

When I found out, all I wanted to do is cry. But I went for a walk and went into the woods and knelt to pray. This is not the story I was told in my last letter from the family. I was told she was hit but would live hopefully with a lot of therapy. Now she was not going to make it through the week. I felt that God was the only one that could calm me down and explain why this had to happen at this time. I trusted the Lord, and I know he had his purpose for me, and he had another mission for me to do at this time and he was telling me it was not time for me to be with another person at this time.

I would find out real soon what he had for me to do. I did still feel it was my obligation to go and see my girlfriend no matter how bad she was. I decided to cut my leave shorter so I could take a few days to go to Louisiana and to see my girl for the last time no matter what condition she was in. I felt I owed her that much and to ask forgiveness for being so rough with her for not writing for such a long time while I was in Vietnam. She, too, was battling to stay alive. I stayed with my family for another week and had a very good reunion making up for lost time.

I got to see a lot of my old school mates, and boy were they ever surprised to see me alive and well. It had hit the papers that I had been killed in action. It seemed as if we had a party every night, and I took center stage. The whole town came out to welcome me home and to thank me for all I had done in Vietnam. How they found out I do not know but they knew. I became a hero to the town and a soldier who had returned from the dead, a first in the history of their town. They said I would be remembered forever.

I left Iowa about a half week later heading for Fort Polk, Louisiana, determined to see my darling girlfriend one last time before she died. I thought up all kinds of situation that I might find her in, but I really hoped I would see her alive, so I could talk to her some. It seemed like the longest ride I had ever taken. I was so quiet on the plane. My neighbor or the one sitting next to me ask me where I was going and why.

I told her my story of Vietnam and my return home. I told her about the call I got about my girlfriend, and I told her I just could not stay away and I had to see her one more time. She told me that she, too, was going to my girlfriend's house because she was a relative and was going to attend the funeral. She said she was happy that I decided to show up and pay respects to Sally again (the name was changed to protect the innocent). I had bought a huge flower arrangement for her. I hoped the parents did not mind.

When I got there, I found out that everyone was at the funeral home. I got dressed in my dress greens with all the metals I had been told I received so far and what was sent to my mother. I looked like a picture from a magazine of a soldier who had been in the service for years and had metals all over the place. When I walked into the funeral home with the lady from the plane, everyone just dropped their jaws. She spoke up and said, "Guess who I meet on the plane here?"

Sally's mother came running and hugged me tight and said, "I knew you would come. You are the bravest man I know and what you have been through. I want to tell the rest about you if I may because you came because you really loved my daughter very much, and I can tell that now. The flowers you sent were her favorite kind, and she has some in her hands. It is a close coffin ceremony, but we will let you take one look after the services if you so desire."

Sally's mother got up and gave a speech of how over four years before Sally and I had met for the first time in church. I was stationed at Fort Polk, Louisiana, for basic training and advanced basic training at Tiger Land. Then I was sent to medical school at Fort Sam Houston, San Antonio, Texas. I then got orders for Vietnam where I spent the last four years plus, two years plus of the four was missing in action. I was exploded out of a jeep on the spring of 1969. I was sent over a mountain six hundred feet down. I was left for dead. I had to live off the land eating what I could find: lizards, snakes, rabbits, worms, dirty water, berries, shrubs that were eatable, and even garbage at times.

All I had was my aid bag and a rucksack on my back, which had a blanket, coat, and rain gear in it and water purification tablets also. I was wounded with a broken collarbone, a separated shoulder, a fractured left knee, and upper leg, shrapnel wounds all over my body, a small caliber bullet hole to the left side of my face going down and tearing out my upper and lower teeth and coming out my lower right jaw. I low crawled through the jungles of Vietnam for over two years, avoiding the enemy patrols in the area with all these injuries I had.

I was able to bandage my injuries with whatever I had in my aid bag or whatever I could find. I hid my sleeping by day and crawled by night. I did many things before I was sent over the mountain, like with what ever material he had in his aid bag or whatever he could to deliver nine babies of Viet Nam birth, and all was under enemy fire. He was shot through his shirt into a book of Mormon, which saved his life because it was right at his heart. I can go on an, on about SSG Swan but look at him, and you can tell that he was and is an extraordinary man. He loved my daughter so much that he sacrificed his wounded body to come here and pay respects to her. I only hope, and pray they will meet again in the eternity, where they can be close friends once again.

Section 7: Went to Fort Dix, New Jersey, and Was Put in Hospital within One Week Because I Was Diagnosed with Malaria Because of Agent Orange and Jungle Fever

It was a very lonely day when I showed up at Fort Dix, New Jersey. The sky was clear, and the birds were flying high overhead. I could smell a different kind of breeze in the air. It made me think of the beach over the South China Sea in Vietnam. Then I got to thinking. It must be the air coming off the ocean for we were not far away. I know Atlantic City is a big tourist trap for people who like to gamble and see the big city. I was assigned to the 556 Ambulance Company. I was reassigned to work in the Aero-Medical Evacuation Section of Lister Army Hospital at Fort Dix, New Jersey.

It did not take long for me to adjust to the work. I was working the night shift the first week, and I had a bad headache, so I went over to the emergency room to try and get some Tylenol or aspirin for my headache. They told me to sit down and they would get to me in just a few minutes. I said I just had a headache and just wanted some aspirin so I could go back to work. They said, "We need to take your temperature. That is the rules here."

They sat me in a chair and put a thermometer in my mouth and in three minutes, took it out. When the nurse read it, she called the doctor. The doctor looked at me and asked if I had been out of country in the past month or so, and I said I just got home from Vietnam. The doctor called for a stretcher bed and an ice blanket. I said, "What is going on? I just have a headache."

The doctor said, "Your temperature is also 104.8 degrees. You are not going nowhere but to an isolation unit for malaria."

They put me in the ice bed and put IVs in my arms and rushed me to the isolation unit. Before we got there, I was out to launch unconscious. I do not remember anything that happened for the next ninety-nine days. I finally woke up, and they told me that I had been out for ninety-nine days. They also told me that they thought that the malaria I had was caused from Agent Orange and jungle fever agents that

I had been in contact with. I might have other problems in the future.

My fever was back to normal, and I felt much better. They also told me that by all rights I should have died, that with a fever that high usually no one comes out of the coma I was in. The doctors said somebody must be really looking out for me.

This is the end of this book about my adventure in the Republic of Vietnam. I went and was missing in action for thirty-four months and labeled killed in action. I was found and put back together. I had to face the fact that my girlfriend was killed instead of me. I did come down with malaria and Agent Orange and jungle fever all in one. There were many more things that Vietnam did that was not mentioned. They will be put in my next book on Vietnam.

CHAPTER 13

Summery of Book

This is my opinion of what this book was all about and why I wrote it to those who will read it. It captures my soul feeling and emotions of my life as a child growing up and how hard it was to cope with society and the elements it took to become a man.

As I became a part of the adult world, I was called upon harshly to serve our country in a very difficult time in my life. I want all those who read this book that I was just a lonely soldier when I got sent to Vietnam. I did not volunteer for the job. I was number one on the draft in our town of Albia, Iowa, back in 1967. I was told by the draft board they would give me twenty-four hours to enlist or be drafted.

I decided to enlist because I would have a choice of which duty I would go into. I liked the idea of medicine, so my choice was the medical field. I do not have anything against the service. I believe every able-bodied young man or woman at the appropriate age should serve their country for at least three years. I do not really believe in the draft except in time of extreme emergencies. Why did I join up into the service can be explained in this poem I wrote just to answer this question!

Why

Duty, honor, and love of country
Is why that I am across the sea
People back home don't understand
Why a boy goes to war and becomes a man.
You ask why your men are here,
In a war-torn country to spend a year.
There is many over here just like me,
Fighting for duty, honor, and love of country!
Can you say the same?

Yes, I am a loyal soldier who was sent to war to spend my year. I did my part, and I did my best. I ended up spending four years in this extremely exhausting jungle crawling on my hand and knees to survive so I could return to be spat on by my own people and called a baby killer. I am proud of every soldier who went to do his part whether it be male or female. They deserve my respect. I am so grateful to our allies, the South Vietnam soldiers and their many different units, the other many countries that volunteered their services to help bring an end to the Vietnam conflict.

The fallen heroes that did not come home, I ask a special blessing to be upon them and their families that they may forever know that their lives they gave will never be forgotten. Yes, I finally made it home, but I will never forget the soldier's in arms that stood beside me, protecting me while I was patching a fellow soldier up so he could be medivac home to his loved ones or the soldiers lying in the trenches with me while we were waiting for air support to cover our position so we could go out and pull in the wounded casualties from harm's way. We all worked as a team, and we supported each other always.

When one was lost, it was a deep cut into us all, but the mission had to go on. To the doctors and nurses who spent relentless hours putting soldiers' lives back together so they could be sent home to their families or a letter written to the family about the loss of their loved ones who would not be coming home alive.

To all though drivers of trucks and jeeps and cooks and laundry people and all those who are not usually thought about as being important in a unit such as a clerk or mail man. I have the upmost respect for you all. It is you that keep the company going and the paperwork moving and the orders going. There are just so many people that are involved in saving one's life. It is unbelievable. I know now that the Good Lord made it possible to send some very remarkable talented people to this earth and placed them in many places on this great earth. God knows what we need and what we need to do to be saved.

If we work together and have true faith in his wisdom and follow him, we can do all thing he has for us to do. This I do believe. This is or what you folks may call here in these United States of America the Land of the Free, the Home of the Brave, your home sweet home. To me, it is my country where I placed my loyalty, integrity, and honor for the past four plus years to protect with almost my life. It is the place I gave my all, to respect the President of this United States of America, and all my family and friends by going to Vietnam as a child and coming back home as a man. To give my full measure and everlasting devotion to our country that we may remain free of sabotage and invasion of our enemies at large.

My next book may get more intense about certain feeling about how things happened and what it really looks like in a war zone. For now, I bit thee ADIEU.

About the Author

Robert Ray Swan is a seventy-one-year-old veteran living in Union, Oregon, with his wife of years. He wrote this book because he was told by his veteran friends and his family and the church that he needs to tell the world that he is still alive and he did make it home from Vietnam and was not killed like the newspapers said he was.

He is not in the best shape and have been through a lot of surgeries by various doctors from Vietnam to surgeons from the Veterans Administration to family practice doctors taking care of him. Surprise! He is still here to tell his story after so many years of therapy and preparation from a lot of doctors and people helping his along the way. He is here to let you know it was not an easy ride to get to this point in his life to tell, but here he is.

CPSIA information can be obtained
at www.ICGtesting.com
Printed in the USA
FSHW021302260122
87922FS